The Frenchwoman's Kitchen

*'In the scrapbooks, the gardens and the kitchens of
family, friends and other instinctive gourmets,
the best traditions of French cuisine are alive and well.'*

The Frenchwoman's Kitchen

BRIGITTE TILLERAY

Photographed by David George

· CASSELL ·

Cassell
Villiers House
41-47 Strand
London WC2N 5JE

Text copyright © Brigitte Tilleray 1990
Volume copyright © Cassell 1990

Distributed in Australia by
Capricorn Link (Australia) Pty Limited,
PO Box 665, Lane Cove, NSW 2066

British Library Cataloguing in Publication Data
Tilleray, Brigitte
The Frenchwoman's kitchen.
1. Food: French regional dishes
I. Title
641.300944

ISBN 0-304-31857-4

Typeset by Litho Link Limited, Welshpool, Powys, Wales
Printed and bound in Spain by Graficas Reunidas

Frontispiece: An early nineteenth-century tiled kitchen.

To all francophiles
and French food enthusiasts

Freshly picked quinces and figs from Gascony.

English Channel

Dunkirk
Calais
Boulogne
Lille
FLANDERS
ARTOIS
THIÉRACHE
ARDENNES
Cherbourg
Le Havre
PICARDY
Caen
NORMANDY
CHAMPAGNE
LORRAINE
ALSACE
Strasbourg
Paris
Isle of Ouessant
Brest
BRITTANY
Seine
BURGUNDY
Loire
VENDÉE
Allier
La Rochelle
CHARENTE-MARITIME
SAINTONGE
POITOU
LIMOUSIN
LYONNAIS
DOMBES
Lyons
AUVERGNE
SAVOIE
PERIGORD
La Puy
Atlantic
Bordeaux
Dordogne
MASSIF
CENTRAL
Lot
ALPS
DRÔME
Rhône
ROUERGUE
Garonne
CAMARGUE
PROVENCE
Nice
Auch
Arles
Bayonne
PAYS
BASQUE
GASCONY
LANGUEDOC
Montpellier
Marseilles
N
PYRÉNÉES
ROUSSILLON
Perpignan
Mediterranean
Cap Corse
CORSICA
Tyrrhenian
Sea
Bastia
Calvi
Vico
Ajaccio
Bonifacio

Contents

Acknowledgements

I express my gratitude to Christopher Fagg, my editor, who gave me the splendid opportunity to rediscover the whole of France. A tour of my homeland without any research assistance seemed an ambitious project at times but overall it was fun and fascinating.

Next I thank David George, photographer, team-mate and navigator for his good humour, and patience, throughout our trips. He captured the day-to-day essence of France with such simplicity – his constant search for the natural, his individual unaffected skill are a complement to the general theme of this book.

I am also extremely grateful to Helen Dore who checked, re-checked – and occasionally refined – my manuscript with enthusiasm and professionalism.

Lastly, a very special thank you to family and friends in France and to the people I hardly knew or did not know at all who so kindly and readily opened their homes and let me share their daily way of life. Without their assistance and willingness the tenor of this book would have been very different.

A farm in the foothills of the Pyrénées

Introduction

From the age of four, allowed by then to spoon the mixture for madeleines into scalloped cake tins – and old enough to be sharply rebuked if I made a mess of it – my earliest recollections are of the careful and loving preparation of food.

The lemony tang of the madeleines was a year-round experience but my recollections of the formative years I spent growing up in a small town in rural France are indelibly associated with the four seasons. Spring is the ultimate freshness of crisp sliced cucumber, summer the splendid ripeness of heavily perfumed, red-fleshed Cavaillon melons. Autumn is the earthy aroma of wild mushrooms and winter the perfume of stored orchard apples unwrapped from tissue paper in warm rooms.

It was good the way we were, before everything became available at all times. It seems unreasonable to decry the cornucopia of today but I wonder if it will produce such exquisite and sharp memories for tomorrow.

My memories are strong indeed. As an only child with parents whose culinary delight in the changing aromas and colours of the seasons was boundless, I believe that I became especially aware of the French national obsession with the pleasures of the table. Obsession? No, I think not. How can something which comes so naturally be described by such an ugly word? So natural it was, and indeed still is in France despite the erosion of a ready-made world. And so totally absorbing . . .

Although I was an only child, my family on both sides is vast. Many are old enough to be steeped still in the true French tradition and many continue that remembered way of life in which cuisine follows the seasons.

Times have changed, but in researching this book over the past year, I found that my France of forty years ago still exists, a little more hidden perhaps, slightly tarnished in places by the speed of life. But in the scrapbooks, the gardens and the kitchens, and above all on the tables of family, friends and other instinctive gourmets who so kindly allowed me to share their way of life, the best traditions are alive and well.

My France is still the France of Guy de Maupassant who wrote in 1887: 'I love this land and I love to live here because this is where my roots are, the deep and delicate roots which bind a man to the earth where his forefathers were born and died, bind him to local customs and local food, to turns of phrase and accents, to the smell of the soil, to the villages and to the air itself.'

With my friend the photographer, David George, I retraced my steps throughout most of the regions of my country to write this book. People generously gave away well-guarded family recipes, many of which I had never come across before. I rediscovered the feeling of France and captured anew the remarkable sensitivity of the French to the land and the preparation of food, and the almost intellectual delight of the French palate.

I was fascinated to rediscover the multi-culture of French cuisine not only by region or season but also through situation, job, craft or profession. Among the miners of the North, the fishermen of Brittany, the farmers of the plains, the grape-pickers of the South, and many more, food is closely linked to tradition.

Perhaps the best summary is once again by Guy de Maupassant, through his character the Docteur de Gournay: 'One is a gourmand just as one is an artist, just as one is cultured, just as one is a poet. The palate is a delicate organ, perceptible and ready to receive, just like the eye or the ear. To have no palate is to be deprived of an exquisite extra sense.'

Autumn pumpkins on a Northern farm ready for the making of warming soups.

CHAPTER 1

The North

ARTOIS · FLANDERS · PICARDY

The harshness of the industrial North hits the traveller at the Channel ports of Calais and Dunkerque. There are no compromises here. Cranes, steelwork and chemical plant chimneys, black mounds of colliery waste and row after row of uninspired city buildings raise their ugly heads against the smoggy sky. It's love-me-or-leave-me country.

But if the visitor chooses to linger, he will be astonished by the other aspects of the North. He will discover not one region but a series of provinces, such as Artois, Flanders and Picardy, as well as ancient towns and rural enclaves he could not dream existed. The landscape varies with the nature of the soil: he will be able to meander along rivers where large-leafed watercress grows wild, and discover jealously guarded rural communities with long farm buildings and whitewashed cottages gathered around squares and village greens.

He will also have time to appreciate the mentality of the Northern French. Whether industrialist, farmer, miner or fisherman, the Northerner may seem undemonstrative at first and certainly lacks southern extravagance, but he is forthright and has a great sense of hospitality. From the devastation of wars to disasters in the collieries or at sea, there have been many occasions when he has had to forgive and forget. The melancholy of the outside world has made him appreciate the quality and warmth of home, and that is where the visitor is always made welcome.

The coffee pot is constantly on the stove. *La bistouille*, a mixture of coffee, chicory and *genièvre*, the local schnapps, is the first offering of friendship. At mealtimes there is local beer: no grapes here, of course, because of the climate, but instead

The industrial North – organic farming near a colliery.

some mean brews with a strong, promising flavour. With it, solid northern dishes making good use of local produce. Among Flanders and Artois specialities are thick vegetable soups, *hochepots* – the French hotpot, a substantial mixture of game or lamb with vegetables – also veal delicately roasted with smoked ham or braised with prunes. Rabbit, both wild and tame, is often on the family menu. It will be prepared either with prunes *à l'artésienne*, stuffed and simmered in beer, or with a mustard and cream sauce. In some households it will be cooked for hours with veal in a well-flavoured stock until the meat falls off the bones, then potted – *le potjeveleish* – and served the following day cold with a mustardy salad of chicory, the indigenous winter vegetable of the north, known locally as *chicon*.

With the proximity of the fishing port of Boulogne and the inland lakes and waterways, a lot of fish is eaten. Herring is a favourite, fresh or smoked into *bouffis*, the prized bloater of the North. Eel is cooked with beer or served cold in aspic, or *au vert*, stewed with the greens of beets and leeks. One of the delicacies of Boulogne is also the small, sweet mussels, served *à la marinières* in huge steaming bowls.

In Picardy, succumb to the most unusual of French accents and do try their *flamique à* z'oignons, a light onion tart, their *tarte à l'pronée*, a prune dessert, or a portion of *l'flamique à l'chitrouille*, a moist pumpkin tart made with the bright orange-fleshed vegetable. *Flamique* is the *patois* word for *flamiche*, the original Flemish name for this light tart made with yeast dough and fruit or vegetables of the season.

I stayed with two sisters in the Thiérache, near Guise, who live what they describe as an old-fashioned way of life. Near St-Omer and further afield in the Avesnois I was invited into two breathtaking kitchens. One was completely lined with handmade Delft tiles, each one with a different pattern, revealing the strong Flemish influence of the region. The other was still in its original Napoleon III style, with stark dark green and white tiles, a precursor of more geometric modern motifs.

In the verdant Vallée de la Course I stopped by the side of the road to buy watercress at a farm and ended up not only eating it with the family but being offered a bed for the night. But my first fascinating stop was at the farm of a chicory grower near Lille . . .

Below: Bloaters: les bouffis du Nord, a Boulogne speciality.

La Perle du Nord

Chicory in English, *endive* in French, *chicon* in northern patois, this pearly white winter vegetable is cultivated exclusively in the North of France. It is just as good cooked as it is raw for salads and makes a pleasant change from all the winter brassica. I was curious to find out how it is grown, so I visited an *endivier* in the mining village of Estevelles, south of Lille.

In the barn women graded the endives into three categories – the top-quality firm white heads, the spindly ones as a second grade and finally the green-leafed inferior quality, slightly bitter but good for cooking. Legs thrust deep into gumboots and a warm scarf around my neck, I followed *mon ami l'endivier* towards the slag heap at the foot of which a whole field of *endive* was laid out.

The vegetable was introduced into France by the Belgians in 1949. Since then, new hybrids have been perfected and the original bitterness of the early plants has gone. I remember the scenes at home when I was forced to eat *endive* as a child. One really needed a gauloise-and-red-wine palate to swallow the bitterness. The cultivation of this vegetable is complex. A root has to be grown first, then butted under a layer of soil, covered and kept warm with straw and metal shields. Within days, the endive will start sprouting from the root. To see them, *en masse*, like some exotic plant against the black soil, is a beautiful sight.

Back at the farm, sipping a warming cup of *bistouille*, we discussed various recipes. Here are some favourites . . .

Opposite: Chicory: cooked or raw in salads – the traditional winter vegetable of Northern France.

Endives au porto

CHICORY BRAISED WITH
SMOKED BACON AND PORT

An excellent accompaniment for any roast fowl or game.

◇

12 heads of chicory
150 g/5 oz butter
12 slices smoked bacon
50 ml/2 fl oz port
pepper

SERVES 6

Wash and trim the chicory. Using a sharp knife, discard some of the core.

Heat the butter in a cast-iron deep pan or flameproof casserole and sauté the bacon slices until they start to brown. Remove from the pan and set aside and sauté the chicory on all sides until golden but not browned. Lay a bacon slice over each head of chicory, add the port and season with freshly ground pepper. Cover and simmer over low heat for 40–45 minutes or until the chicory feels tender all the way through. Turn the vegetables once or twice during cooking. If necessary, add a little lukewarm water to the cooking juices. Transfer the chicory to a heated serving dish and spoon over the stock and port.

Pintade à la flamande

GUINEA FOWL BRAISED WITH CHICORY

100 g/4 oz butter
2 teaspoons sunflower oil
3 slices unsmoked streaky bacon
1 guinea fowl
2 carrots, chopped
3 shallots, finely chopped
1 bouquet garni
1 kg/2 lb chicory
juice of 1 lemon
salt and pepper

SERVES 4

Heat half the butter and the oil in a flameproof casserole. Brown the bacon and set aside. Seal the guinea fowl on all sides until slightly brown. Take out of the casserole and sauté the carrots and shallots until transparent. Place the guinea fowl over this bed of vegetables, add the bouquet garni and cover the bird with the bacon slices. Cover and cook over low heat for 45 minutes, turning the guinea fowl once or twice.

Meanwhile, wash and dry the chicory. Slice into thick, even slices, discarding the cores. Melt the remaining butter in a deep sauté pan. Add the chicory and toss well with a wooden spatula, making sure the butter does not brown. Add a little water and the lemon juice. Season. Cover and simmer over low heat for 30 minutes.

Five minutes before serving, arrange the cooked chicory around the guinea fowl in the casserole. Toss the vegetables in the cooking juices. Cover and simmer for 5 minutes.

Take the bird out of the casserole. Carve and transfer to a heated serving platter. Discard the bouquet garni, arrange the vegetables around the guinea fowl and spoon the cooking juices over the whole dish. Serve at once.

Endives farcies braisées

BRAISED CHICORY WITH
A MUSHROOM AND CHICKEN FILLING

6 firm heads of chicory
225 g/8 oz chicken breast, minced
225 g/8 oz freshly ground pork
50 g/2 oz mushrooms, chopped
2 parsley sprigs, chopped
2 shallots, finely chopped
1 egg, beaten
salt and pepper
6 slices smoked streaky bacon
½ teaspoon tomato purée
200 ml/7 fl oz white wine

SERVES 6

Preheat the oven to 200°C/400°F/gas mark 6.

Wash and dry the chicory. Bring a pan of salted water to the boil and blanch the chicory for 8 minutes. Drain well in a colander, run quickly under a cold tap, and leave to cool.

Prepare the stuffing by mixing together the chicken and pork with the mushrooms, parsley, shallots, the egg, salt and pepper. Gently open the

A kitchen in the Avesnois – hand-painted tiles reveal the Flemish traditions of the region.

chicory leaves and spoon some of the stuffing inside each head. Close the stuffed vegetable into its original shape. Wrap each one with a bacon slice and place in a single layer in a baking dish.

Bake in the preheated oven for 15 minutes on one side, then turn the chicory, add the tomato purée mixed with the wine and bake for a further 15 minutes until the bacon is golden all over. If necessary add a little warm water to the bottom of the dish, to prevent the chicory from sticking. Cover the dish with foil, reduce the oven temperature to 180°C/350°F/gas mark 4 and cook for a further 40 minutes. Serve with creamed potatoes and the cooking juices.

The Watercress Valley

I left the endive farm and drove towards the coast . . . When travelling from Boulogne to Montreuil, leave the monotonous main road and follow the small lanes to the Vallée de la Course. The immediate contrast in the landscape is surprising. The river runs fast through watermeadows with gravel paths and ancient bridges. From time to time the shimmer of a trout's back teases the water surface. All along the river's course, through narrow hamlets and past plain country churches, wide-leafed watercress abounds.

It was on an afternoon walk between Beussent and Pont Terratu that I spotted the large bunches of watercress for sale on a garden chair. As I approached, a dark-haired woman dressed *à la paysanne* in a charcoal calico wrapover was knee-deep in the river, cutting and bunching. She turned round and addressed me in a Picard accent so strong, it took me a while to adjust. I bought some watercress and we started talking. We talked more and I was invited into her house. An hour later I was urged to join the family for supper – I accepted, and, after a meal of watercress, cider and more watercress I retired to an upstairs room because 'it was too late for a young woman on her own to go and find lodgings'. This must be the finest example of Northern hospitality.

We ate our evening meal in the main room – a small kitchen was adjacent. The savoury aroma of watercress perfumed the atmosphere. We started with a tureen of watercress soup brought piping hot to the table, then a fried pork chop served with a purée of dried peas and fresh watercress. We finished this *repas du coeur* with a *rabote Picarde*, a fragrant apple wrapped and baked inside a fine sheet of puff pastry.

Soupe campagnarde au cresson

THICK WATERCRESS SOUP

1 large bunch of watercress
3 onions
2 large potatoes
50 g/2 oz butter
750 ml/1¼ pints water
salt
2 teaspoons thick *crème fraîche*

SERVES 4

Wash the watercress and chop the leaves and stems finely. Peel and chop the onions. Peel, wash and dice the potatoes.

Heat the butter in a large saucepan and as it melts toss in the onions and sauté until transparent, then add the watercress. Add the potatoes and water. Add salt, cover the pan and simmer for 20 minutes or until the potatoes are cooked. Check the seasoning, add the *crème fraîche*, stir well and serve at once without blending.

Purée picarde

PURÉE OF DRIED PEAS
AND FRESH WATERCRESS

350 g/12 oz dried peas
4 tablespoons milk
1 large knob butter
2 heaped tablespoons finely chopped watercress leaves
2 hard-boiled eggs

SERVES 4

Soak the peas for one hour in lukewarm water. Rinse well and cook until tender in boiling water. Drain well and push through a sieve until a thick purée is formed.

Return the purée to the saucepan and add the milk. Lower the heat as far as possible and leave the purée to dry and thicken, stirring from time to time as it has a tendency to adhere to the bottom of the pan. Just before serving mix in the butter and the watercress and then garnish with slices of hard-boiled egg.

To serve with pork chops: Fry the chops in a little butter until cooked. Transfer the chops to a serving platter and pour the pan juices over the vegetable purée.

—— A Napoleon III *Gentilhommière* ——

If I had not visited Madame Dupont in her early nineteenth-century gentleman's country residence, I would never have come upon the natural beauty of the *campagne Andomaroise*. I would also never have had the pleasure of sharing a complete Flemish birthday meal cooked by Robert le Flamand. And all this only a few kilometres away from the industrial sites of Calais where after the cobbled market town of Ardres the landscape gives way to hills, valleys and, towards St-Olmer, a network of forests, lakes and waterways.

There, in the morning mist, the market gardener or the early fisherman slowly makes his way through the maze of fens and dykes on a solid flat punt called a *bacove* – the only way to gather the garden yield or to bring home a pike, zander, eel, perch or trout.

In the autumn wildfowl abounds. Then, the hunter and his retriever will walk the paths in search of something for the pot.

Robert had chosen wild rabbit for the meal he cooked in his friend's kitchen at Bonningues-les-Ardres. The house is set in formal grounds, a classic building with original black-and-white floors, moulded ceilings and carved fireplaces. In the kitchen, the floor is made of small flagstones and the tiling between this room and the adjacent scullery is quite baroque.

All the copper pots and pans were out, there was not a free surface anywhere – a man was in the process of creating a culinary *chef-d'oeuvre*. A home-made chicken stock had finished simmering, cauliflowers were trimmed and cut into florets for a *velouté de chou-fleur* – a smooth *potage* delicate in both taste and texture. A rich aroma came from the large copper pot on the stove in which the rabbit was simmering in a sauce made of beer and blackcurrant juice. Apples were cored, filled with raspberries, sprinkled with raspberry-flavoured beer and placed in the oven to bake. 'Is this the dessert?' I asked. 'No, no, no,' said the cook, 'it is part of the main course. It will be magnificent, just wait and see,' he added. Somehow I felt this was not the time to ask for the recipe and retired to another room until the maestro called for help to take the first course through.

The meal was exquisitely prepared and the potency of the fruit-flavoured beers combined with rich sauces and the wine all contributed to an evening of immense joviality.

Above: Original tiling in a Napoleon III-period kitchen.

Opposite: Among brass and copper utensils, a fifteenth-century meat-safe.

Velouté de chou-fleur

— CAULIFLOWER SOUP —

1 cauliflower
600 ml/1 pint well-flavoured chicken stock
300 ml/½ pint milk
2 teaspoons cornflour
125 ml/4 fl oz thick *crème fraîche*
1 heaped tablespoon finely chopped chervil

— SERVES 4-6 —

Separate the cauliflower into florets and cook in plenty of salted boiling water. Drain well and add to the chicken stock. Blend smoothly in an electric blender and return to the pan with most of the milk. Make a paste with the remaining cold milk and cornflour, add to the soup and stirring constantly over a gentle heat, let it thicken. Add the *crème fraîche* and chervil. Stir for a few minutes and serve at once.

Lapin à la Flamande

— RABBIT COOKED IN BEER —
— AND FRESH BLACKCURRANT JUICE —

It is essential to use the juice of fresh blackcurrants, for the sharpness is the key to the flavour of the finished dish.

◇

1 large rabbit
25 g/1 oz butter
1 tablespoon sunflower oil
100 g/4 oz smoked bacon, diced into *lardons*
500 g/1 lb small onions, sliced
1 × 750 ml/1¼ pint bottle brown ale
200 ml/7 fl oz unsweetened blackcurrant juice
salt and pepper
1 bouquet garni
1 tablespoon thick *crème fraîche*
Baked apples *(recipe follows)*

— SERVES 6 —

Cut the rabbit into 8 pieces. Heat the butter and oil in a flameproof casserole and brown the rabbit pieces on all sides. Remove from the pan and sauté the lardons and onions together until golden-brown. Add the beer and blackcurrant juice, salt, pepper and bouquet garni.

Return the rabbit pieces to the casserole, cover and simmer for 1½ hours or until very tender. If necessary add a little lukewarm water to the sauce halfway through the cooking time.

To serve, transfer the rabbit to a heated deep serving dish. Add the *crème fraîche* to the sauce, bring quickly to the boil and spoon over the rabbit. Serve garnished with a baked apple per person.

Pommes à la flamande

— BAKED APPLES —

To be prepared with French or Belgian raspberry-flavoured beer. If not available, add 4 tablespoons raspberry juice to a bottle of lager-type beer.

◇

6 medium cooking apples, peeled and cored
100 g/4 oz frozen raspberries
6 teaspoons brown sugar
50 g/2 oz butter
1 × 750 ml/1¼ pint bottle raspberry-flavoured beer

— SERVES 6 —

Preheat the oven to 200°C/400°F/gas mark 6.

Arrange the apples in a baking dish. Place a few raspberries inside each one. Sprinkle with the sugar. Divide the butter among the apples. Bake in the preheated oven for 15 minutes, then sprinkle with the beer and continue baking until the apples are tender but not mushy. Add another sprinkling of beer if necessary.

—— An Old-fashioned Way of Life ——

I left the black North through southern Picardy and the Thiérache, a lush northern enclave known as *la petite Normandie* where the apple trees grow wild among the wooded hills, and – dominated by the earliest Gothic cathedral in France at the medieval town of Laon – each village claims its own fortified church.

There I visited Mesdemoiselles Piette, two spinster sisters, exquisitely *vieille France*, who pride themselves in being immersed in an old-fashioned way of life. Devoted to their faith, their family and friends, they live a contented life of intellectual self-sufficiency, making no concession to age.

When their pharmacist parents died, they decided to open the eighteenth-century family home to tourists, and from their gleaming and pristine kitchen at the heart of the house they devote themselves to the comfort and well-being of their guests. The kitchen garden boasts every organically grown vegetable and herb available to prepare fresh meals throughout the four seasons. Cheese comes from the local farm and so does the cider. The sisters do not eat much meat and if chicken is served it is free range. They happily trot from kitchen to dining-room attending to every detail and will take dessert with their guests, accompanied by a good wine poured from an antique crystal decanter.

The evening I spent with them was fascinating, the conversation lively and the food and recipes another source of information about a region with which I was not too familiar. After a *potage de légumes du jardin*, a refreshing thin but very vegetably soup, we were served a hot tart made with Maroilles, one of the famous cheeses of France, invented centuries ago by monks at the Abbaye of nearby Maroilles and made throughout the Thiérache and Avesnois. Pungent, of supple texture, it in fact tastes quite mild and cooks into a tangy paste.

The third course was a *poulet au cidre*, a fricassee of free-range chicken subtly simmered with herbs and cider without the addition of onion or garlic. It was served with the local *boulettes a pemmes ed' terre* – a kind of potato cake – and a green salad.

When *les Demoiselles* joined us for dessert, they brought in a *tarte à l'pronée*, a sharp prune tart made with a fine *pâte brisée* and served lukewarm.

Tarte au maroilles
des Demoiselles Piette

──── MAROILLES CHEESE TART ────

The quantities indicated below
will make 2 tarts.

◇

PÂTE LEVÉE (YEAST DOUGH)
15 g/½ oz fresh yeast
2 tablespoons lukewarm milk
500 g/1 lb plain flour
100 g/4 oz unsalted butter, finely diced
a pinch of salt
40 g/1½ oz sugar
3 eggs

FILLING
100 g/4 oz Maroilles cheese
25 g/1 oz butter
2 eggs
225 g/8 oz full-fat *fromage blanc*
salt and pepper
nutmeg

──────── SERVES 6 ────────

Crumble the yeast into the milk in a small bowl. Mash with a fork and leave in a warm place for 15 minutes.

Using the fingertips, combine the flour, butter, salt and sugar on a large wooden board. Make a well in the centre. Break in the eggs and pour in the yeast mixture. Using the fingertips, work the central ingredients together first, then draw in the flour. Knead the dough for 10 minutes or until elastic. Leave to prove in a warm room for 2 hours.

Knead once more to knock out the air and using the knuckles of your hands flatten the dough into a 23 cm/9 inch tart dish.

Preheat the oven to 200°C/400°F/gas mark 6.

To make the filling, discard the cheese rind. Dot thin slices of cheese and butter over the dough. Separate the eggs. Whisk the whites until stiff. Beat the yolks with the fromage blanc, add salt, pepper and freshly grated nutmeg and fold in the egg whites. Pour the mixture over the dough. Bake in the preheated oven for 45 minutes or until the filling is firm and golden and the pastry is cooked.

The gleaming kitchen at the Demoiselles Piette.

Poulet au cidre du Thiérache

CHICKEN FRICASSEE WITH DRY CIDER

1.5 kg/3 lb farm chicken
25 g/1 oz margarine
6 fresh sage leaves
1 bayleaf
2 fresh thyme sprigs
200 ml/7 fl oz dry cider
salt and pepper

SERVES 4–6

Cut the chicken into 8 pieces. Melt the margarine in a cast iron or flameproof casserole and sauté the chicken pieces on all sides until brown. Add the herbs and cider and season with salt and pepper. Reduce the heat and simmer, covered, for 1 hour or until the chicken is tender. Serve with pan juices spooned over the chicken.

Boulettes à pemmes ed'terre

SMALL POTATO CAKES

250 g/9 oz freshly boiled potatoes, mashed
1 heaped tablespoon finely chopped onion
40 g/1½ oz butter, melted
salt and pepper
25 g/1 oz plain flour
extra butter and oil, for frying

SERVES 4–6

Mix the potato, onion, butter and seasoning in a bowl. Gradually add the flour until a soft dough is formed. Roll into even-sized balls and sauté on all sides in a mixture of hot oil and butter.

La tarte à l'pronée

PRUNE TART

PASTRY
200 g/7 oz plain flour
90 g/3½ oz unsalted butter
1 egg yolk
a little iced water

FILLING
250 g/9 oz prunes, stoned
1 vanilla pod, split open
100 g/4 oz sugar

SERVES 6

Soak the prunes in water. Cook them with a little water and the vanilla pod until tender. Leave to cool. Meanwhile, make the pastry. Sift the flour on to a wooden board and make a well in the centre. Dot small pieces of butter over the flour. Add the egg yolk to the well and, using the fingertips, draw in the flour and butter until a dough is formed, adding a little iced water to bind, if necessary. Leave the pastry to rest for 45–50 minutes.

Preheat the oven to 200°F/400°C/gas mark 6.

Line a 23 cm/9 inch tart dish with the thinly rolled out pastry. Spoon the drained prunes into the pastry case. Sprinkle the sugar over the fruit and bake in the preheated oven for 30 minutes or until the pastry is cooked and crisp. Serve lukewarm or cold.

— CHAPTER 2 —

Normandy

Normandy follows the seasons just as a woman follows the natural stages of her life cycle. Sensuality is her secret weapon, from the bridal blossoming of spring to the soft, natural opulence of summer, followed by the fruitful ripeness of autumn; and, when the field has fallen fallow, nowhere does the soft landscape unite more readily with the shrouding winter sky.

In keeping with the femininity of the landscape, pretty homes are scattered all over the Norman countryside. Long black and white half-timbered *chaumières*, their thatched roofs planted with irises, beautiful farmhouses of stone and soft pink brick and, in the Contentin, pale grey stone buildings and manor houses adorned with turrets and dormer-windows. Almost every village has its château, a reminder that this region is one of the last bastions of French aristocracy; some of the large local families descend directly from the Dukes of Normandy. They are mostly landowners and, with the farmers, exploit this rich land to the full. The quality of the grass provides Norman livestock with excellent nourishment and along the sands of the Cotentin coast, down to the Mont-St-Michel, sheep are left to graze the salty sea grass. Ducks, large brown hens and guinea fowl are familiar sights in the Norman farmyard. If the climate does not allow the growth of southerly vegetables such as peppers or aubergines, the soil, gorged with sea air and seaweed, is an excellent propagator for the more common vegetables. Cabbages, carrots and leeks as well as early peas, beans and hearty salad greens flourish there.

Along the coast, shrimpers fish daily the small *crevette grise*, and every morning trawlers return to the numerous fishing ports, Le Tréport, Dieppe, Fécamp, Honfleur or Cherbourg, with heavy loads of soles, turbot, whiting, tiny mackerel and herrings – all caught strictly according to the season. Crab is small and sweet; so are the tiny blue mussels and the pink langoustines.

In this land of plenty, species of fruit long forgotten in a more commercially minded world adorn the boughs of the Normandy orchard. Cherries in June along the river Seine, then a multitude of old-fashioned pears and apples. The eating apple and the sharp indigenous 'cider apple' are essentially the fruit of Normandy.

The riches of the land dictate the riches of the table. Among the traditional dishes of Normandy it is *de rigueur* to mention *tripes à la mode de Caen*, a dish of tripe and calf's foot which is left to simmer for days on the stove. Cooked with carrots, onions, herbs and cider, it is often the farmer's breakfast during the colder months. Regional *charcuterie* is good, and the Norman housewife will often serve *boudin noir*, a light black pudding oozing with cream, and at Christmas-time, *boudin blanc*, a delicate white pudding made of chicken breast, herbs, cream and truffles. It is traditionally eaten in every household as a second course in the Christmas Eve midnight supper.

Autumn in Normandy – 'nowhere does the soft landscape unite more readily with the sky.'

The essential ingredient of the cuisine of Normandy has to be the thick, hand-churned, slightly sour cream – *crème fraîche* – which can be purchased from farmers' wives in most market places. It is the natural accompaniment to chicken in *poule au blanc*, as well as to white fish, root and green vegetables. Real Norman *crème fraîche* is made with unpasteurized milk and left to thicken and develop its sharp tang naturally. The pasteurized version may now be purchased anywhere. It is reflavoured by the addition of a lactic bacteria but its quality is very much disputed among the true connoisseurs of *crème fraîche normande*.

Cheeses of the region, each with its individual taste and texture, are renowned worldwide. Consider Camembert, Pont-Lévêque, Livarot, all matured to creamy softness.

Like the landscape, like the seasons, the cuisine of Normandy is a mélange of soft nuances. Its best example is probably the unparalleled flavour of the freshly churned butter I tasted for breakfast at an old schoolfriend's farm last spring . . .

Left: A working farm in the Norman countryside.

Spring in Normandy

—— Butter Making at a Normandy Farm ——

It is May and the world is in bloom. Yesterday it rained all day, a soft drizzle very characteristic of the region. This morning, since the early clouds dispersed, the Norman spring countryside belongs once more to the world of the Impressionists.

I have spent the night at a friend's house near my native town of Yvetot. Her farmhouse, like so many in the region, stands at the centre of an apple orchard at the end of a grass-banked lane. The trees are heavy with blossom this year and in a few months' time the crabbed waxy fruits will exude their pungent perfume over the fields. Gallons of cider will be made and with the mashings, while he still holds the rights to distil, my friend's husband will make his fabled Calvados, known to all for its dramatic after-effects.

Today is butter-making day. My friends have been up long before me to milk the cows, make today's cream and, as on every Friday, prepare the few kilos of butter which will be sold tomorrow in the market, together with thick cream and dozens of free-range eggs. At this time of the year, the quality of the grass is exceptional, the milk is rich, and the traditionally made Normandy butter has no equal. To have the opportunity of taking it straight from the dairy to the kitchen table for breakfast is very special: no jam is needed, no seasoning, just the nutty flavour of the creamy, hand-churned butter thickly spread on fresh slices of crusty country bread.

Brigitte inherited her farmhouse from her grandparents and to her great joy all the antique

Left: Separating the cream.

Right: Freshly churned butter and antique box-wood butter pat.

Norman furniture which was already in it, along with a rare and splendid collection of antique butter moulds. The kitchen is quintessentially a country kitchen. It contains nothing fitted or modern but instead the waxy scent of a huge ornate sideboard, *le buffet campagnard*, the soft murmur of an old cast-iron kettle kept warm on the enamelled stove inside a blue-and-white tiled fireplace, a glittering copper jam pan, old crockery and crisp pleated gingham.

In these rustic surroundings my friend lives the traditional life of a farmer's wife. Holidays are unknown and as a farm can never be left unattended we all rally round, lend a hand and spend marvellous days being regally entertained. Brigitte is an excellent cook. I spent a week with her this time, cooking and sampling the recipes that her grandmother had so religiously left in her careful handwriting on the top shelf of the old *buffet*. They were all excellent.

ramekins. Brown them in the remaining butter in a frying pan.

When the eggs are set, place a croûton of bread in the centre of individual plates. Turn the egg from each ramekin on to the bread. Sprinkle the chopped parsley over the eggs and spoon the cream sauce around.

Maquereaux ou harengs marinés dieppoise

— SOUSED MACKEREL OR HERRING —

When the mackerel and herring season starts, the small fish are firm and sold on Dieppe market in great profusion. They are delicious soused. With crusty bread and a bottle of dry Normandy cider they make a delectable simple lunch and are a seasonal tradition *sur la table normande*.

◇

12 small mackerel or herrings
4 carrots, thinly sliced
4 onions, thinly sliced
salt
2 cloves
2 bayleaves
a few sprigs of thyme
2 teaspoons black and white peppercorns, mixed
4 slices of lemon
400 ml/14 fl oz water
200 ml/7 fl oz dry white wine
125 ml/4 fl oz cider vinegar

— SERVES 6 —

Clean the fish and wash it thoroughly under the cold tap. Cover the base of a deep, oblong, flameproof dish with half the carrots, onions, salt, herbs and peppercorns. Lay the fish carefully on top, side by side, repeat and finish with a layer of lemon slices. Mix the water, wine and vinegar together and pour over the fish.

Cover the dish, bring to the boil and simmer for 10–15 minutes according to the size of the fish. Leave to cool and place in a cold room or at the base of the refrigerator for at least 3 days before serving.

To serve, lift each fish from the stock with a fish slice, garnish with a few slices of pickled carrots and onions and a little stock. Eat very well chilled.

Oeufs brayons

— BAKED EGGS —

A delicious first course, excellent made with duck eggs. Make sure they are very fresh.

◇

6 eggs
9 tablespoons *crème fraîche*
salt and pepper
200 g/7 oz unsalted butter
6 thin slices of bread
3 teaspoons finely chopped fresh parsley

— SERVES 6 —

Preheat the oven to 180°C/350°F/gas mark 4.

Beat the eggs with 3 tablespoons of *crème fraîche*, salt and pepper. Grease with butter the inside of 6 individual ramekin dishes. Divide the egg mixture among the dishes. Stand them in a pan of water and bake in the preheated oven for 10 minutes or until just set.

Meanwhile, make a sauce by slowly melting half of the remaining butter and all the remaining *crème fraîche* with a little salt and plenty of black pepper. Stir well and thicken over low heat, stirring constantly, until the sauce coats the back of the spoon. Cut the bread into 6 circles the size of

Poisson aux câpres, sauce normande

—— FISH WITH CAPERS IN NORMANDY SAUCE ——

Fish poached in a *court-bouillon* with a cream and caper sauce. A succulent way of preparing any white fish, the ritual Friday meal in Normandy. Replace the capers with a few shrimps, and/or shelled mussels and you have a *poisson à la diéppoise*. It is all wonderfully simple.

◇

1.5 kg/3 lb firm white fish

COURT-BOUILLON
2 litres/3½ pints water
400 ml/14 fl oz dry cider
1 onion, studded with a clove
1 carrot
2 small leeks
1 teaspoon black and white peppercorns, mixed
1 tablespoon cider vinegar
1 bouquet garni

SAUCE NORMANDE
50 g/2 oz unsalted butter
225 ml/8 fl oz *crème fraîche*
freshly ground sea salt
freshly ground pepper

—— SERVES 6 ——

The best way to cook the fish is to prepare a strong cider *court bouillon*. Lower the fish in, either whole or in slices, and simmer gently until the fish just flakes. Never overcook fish, it toughens when cooked for too long.

Bring all the ingredients to the boil and boil for 15 minutes. Leave to cool, then lower the fish into the *court-bouillon*, bring to a gentle simmer and cook until just done.

Place the butter and *crème fraîche* in a small saucepan. Season with salt and pepper. Warm slowly, stirring constantly, until the sauce thickens and coats the back of the spoon.

(Half a jar of drained capers or/and 225 g/8 oz shellfish, such as shrimps or prawns, may also be added to the sauce.)

To serve, skin the fish and transfer to a heated serving platter or individual plates. Spoon the *sauce normande* over it.

Opposite: Brigitte's rustic kitchen near Yvetot.

Right: On the quay at Dieppe.

Légumes à la normande

—— VEGETABLES NORMANDY-STYLE ——

◇

The *Sauce normande (see previous recipe)* is also traditionally made to accompany vegetables. I use it for new potatoes, haricot beans, salsify, green beans, cauliflower and spinach, or serve it separately in a sauce boat with asparagus. It is smoother and lighter than just melted butter. Always sprinkle on a good amount of fresh chopped parsley before serving.

Harengs du Havre

—— BAKED HERRINGS ——

Stuffed with mixed soft and hard roes, these are served with buttered new potatoes and nothing else.

◇

3 herrings with soft roe
3 herrings with hard roe
1 teaspoon softened unsalted butter
2 purple shallots, finely chopped
2 teaspoons finely chopped parsley
50 g/2 oz mushrooms, finely chopped
salt and pepper
a little sunflower oil

—— SERVES 6 ——

Preheat the oven to 190°C/375°F/gas mark 5.

Using a fork, mash the soft and hard roes to a paste with the butter and all the other ingredients except the oil. Spoon this mixture inside the cavity of each fish. Lay the fish in an oblong baking dish and, brush each with a little oil. Cover with kitchen foil and bake in the preheated oven for 15–20 minutes according to the size of the fish.

Le pâté de poisson

— FISH PÂTÉ —

A cold fish pâté – the addition of tomato purée makes it taste almost like lobster. Serve cold with a lemon mayonnaise. The pâté can be made one or two days in advance and kept in the refrigerator.

◇

750 g/1½ lb any firm white fish
5 eggs, beaten
2 teaspoons tomato purée
salt and pepper
butter for greasing

— SERVES 6 —

Poach the fish in a *Court-bouillon* (*see page 00*). Leave it to cool in the stock. When cold, lift the fish from the stock, draining well. Skin it and discard all the bones.

Mash the fish coarsely in a mixing bowl. Add the eggs, tomato purée and seasoning.

Preheat the oven to 180°C/350°F/gas mark 4. Butter a Pyrex or china loaf tin, pack the mixture into it, and stand in a pan of warm water. Bake in the preheated oven for 45 minutes. Leave to cool in the tin.

To serve, cut the pâté into thick slices and accompany with home-made mayonnaise.

Lapin à l'oseille

— RABBIT IN A SORREL SAUCE —

1 rabbit
50 g/2 oz unsalted butter
25 g/1 oz plain flour
salt and pepper
450 ml/¾ pint chicken stock
500 g/1 lb sorrel
2 egg yolks
150 ml/5 fl oz *crème fraîche* or double cream

— SERVES 6 —

Divide the rabbit into portions. Heat the butter in a flameproof casserole and sauté the rabbit on all sides until it is just golden brown. Sprinkle the flour over the meat. Mix well and leave to colour for 2 minutes. Add seasoning and cover with the stock. Bring to the boil, then lower the heat and cook for 45 minutes or until the rabbit pieces start to feel very tender, turning the pieces in the sauce from time to time.

Wash and chop the sorrel. Add to the rabbit, mix well with a wooden spoon and simmer, uncovered, for a further 15 minutes.

To make the sauce, put the egg yolks into a small mixing bowl and whisk in the *crème fraîche*. Using a slotted spoon, lift the rabbit pieces from the sauce and transfer to a serving dish. Keep warm.

Beat 2 large serving spoons of the stock into the egg and cream mixture, pour it into the casserole, and using a hand whisk stir the sorrel sauce over a very low heat for 5 minutes or until it is thick enough to coat the back of a spoon. Check the seasoning. Spoon over the rabbit pieces and serve at once with steamed new potatoes.

Poule au blanc

— CHICKEN IN CREAM SAUCE —

One reads of various recipes for chicken cooked in a cream sauce, sometimes with Calvados as in *poulet vallée d'Auge*. But the original recipe for *poule au blanc* is an old Normandy dish and I was not surprised to find it in Brigitte's grandmother's recipe book.

It is essential to use a boiling fowl; the taste of the stock obtained is so much more flavoursome. It is also very difficult to give a cooking time as it all depends on the age of the bird. It will be cooked when the top of the thigh feels tender when pricked with a skewer.

◇

50 g/2 oz unsalted butter
1 heaped tablespoon plain flour
water
1 boiling fowl
6 large carrots
3 leeks, tied together
2 turnips
4 onions, one studded with a clove
1 bouquet garni
400 ml/14 fl oz dry cider
salt and pepper
2 egg yolks
250 ml/8 fl oz *crème fraîche*

— SERVES 6 OR MORE —

Make a light roux by melting together the butter and flour at the bottom of a large pan. Add a little

Small churns are used daily to fetch milk from the farm.

Tourte normande aux poires

— SPICY PEAR PIE —

A spicy pear pie laced with cream at the last minute.

◇

PÂTE BRISÉE
225 g/8 oz plain flour
100 g/4 oz unsalted butter
a pinch of salt
3 tablespoons iced water

FILLING
600 g/1¼ lb firm perfumed pears
3 tablespoons Calvados
a pinch of black pepper
100 g/4 oz caster sugar
1 egg yolk mixed with a little water, for glazing
150 ml/5 fl oz *crème fraîche*

— SERVES 4–6 —

water, whisk to a paste with a hand whisk, then add more water until the liquid is smooth and free of lumps. Place the bird inside the pot with the vegetables and bouquet garni. Add the cider and cover with water. Bring to the boil quickly, skim the surface with a skimming ladle, reduce the heat, season, cover and cook gently until the chicken is tender. It could take up to 3 hours.

To make the sauce, first of all skim as much fat as possible from the surface of the chicken stock. Carve the chicken into large pieces and place in a heated deep serving dish.

Put the egg yolks in a mixing bowl and beat in the *crème fraîche*. Pour one ladleful of chicken stock into the bowl, whisk with a hand whisk. Add two more ladlesful. If you think more sauce is needed add a little more stock. Pour into a saucepan and stir constantly over very low heat until the sauce is thick enough to coat the back of a spoon. Pour over the chicken. Lift the carrots out of the stock, slice and serve them with a green vegetable and a few steamed potatoes.

The remaining stock will make a delicious chicken consommé: strain it through a fine sieve and reheat with very fine pasta. Or keep frozen or refrigerated to use in other recipes whenever chicken stock is needed.

Make the pastry and leave to rest in a cool place for 2 hours. Peel the pears and slice fairly thickly. Leave to macerate for 30 minutes in the Calvados, black pepper and 75 g/3 oz of the caster sugar.

Drain the pear slices with a slotted spoon and reserve the marinade.

Preheat the oven to 200°C/400°F/gas mark 6.

Roll out two-thirds of the pastry dough 5 mm/¼ inch thick. Use to line a 25 cm/10 inch decorative pie dish (which you will take to the table). Leave a rim of pastry overlapping at the top. Prick the pastry with a fork, fill the dish with the drained pears and sprinkle with the remaining sugar. Roll out the remaining dough and use to cover the pie, trimming the edges and pressing together well.

Glaze the surface of the pie with the egg and water mix. Cut a small hole in the centre of the pastry and insert either a china pie funnel or a piece of foil or folded cardboard.

Bake in the preheated oven for 40 minutes. In a small saucepan, reduce the pear and Calvados juice slightly, add the *crème fraîche* and stir until warm, without boiling. Gently pour through the pie funnel and leave to cool slightly. Serve the pie lukewarm, straight from the dish.

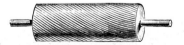

—— Luncheon at the Old Priory – *Les Deux Curés* ——

My French home is an ancient limestone priory set at the top of a hill among the green patchwork of the Contentin *bocage*. The childhood home of Guy de Maupassant's grandfather who, as an orphan, was brought up there by his godfather, a priest, it seems to have been inhabited over the years by some intrepid ecclesiasts, one of whom had to leave the long robe after insisting on the employment of a young maid when the rules of the clergy stipulated that a priest's female servant should be over forty years old.

Although in the winter fires in the large Evreux stone hearths are lit from dawn in each room of this rambling house built around a courtyard, the kitchen is for many obvious reasons its focal point. Opening straight on to a path leading to a *potager*, a large vegetable garden which stocks the stewpot all year round, the kitchen door is flanked by an old water pump from which runs fresh spring water. From my indispensable 'Paul Bocuse' back-tiled stove set under a broad half-timbered period hood, many meals have been prepared.

As *noblesse oblige*, two of my very first visitors there were distant cousins, and brothers at that, who both decided to embrace the Faith and are in charge of small parishes in the Calvados region. Deprived by design of some other earthly pleasures, my *curé* cousins are great trenchermen and a meal

shared with them would be hard to match for an occasion of agreeable gourmandising.

We started with an *omelette normande aux crevettes*, made with the freshest of shrimps I had cooked that morning. To follow, as the Contentin is the land of the *pré salé* – salt marsh lamb – we consumed a solid *terrinée de gigot à l'ancienne*, a braised dish of lamb, beans and potatoes. Then, after a well-deserved rest and the ceremonial passing round of the Calvados bottle for the *trou normand* – to help the digestion, as the Norman saying goes – we had a salad made of *doucette*, the local name for lamb's lettuce, a few dandelions and fine slivers of locally smoked raw ham in a chopped hazelnut dressing.

In true Norman tradition we drank cider all through the meal, our own dry cider from one of the six barrels carefully resting in the *ciderie* adjacent to the house. But to obey the rules, one or two – I really cannot remember – bottles of *vieux Bourgogne* were drunk with the cheeses: a sumptuous farm Camembert *au lait cru* made at the farm below and, of course, as a must for our guests a piece of *Trappe*, a cheese made by the monks in our nearby town of Bricquebec.

For dessert I served a chilled apple aspic with an earthenware jar full of the slightly tangy local *crème fraîche*.

Opposite: A Contentin stone manor house.

Above: The old water pump.

Omelette normande aux crevettes

SHRIMP OMELETTE

150 g/5 oz cooked shelled shrimp
1 tablespoon *crème fraîche*
white pepper
4 fresh tarragon leaves, finely chopped
6 large eggs
1 tablespoon single cream
50 g/2 oz unsalted butter

SERVES 4

In a bowl mix the shrimps with the *crème fraîche*, the pepper and tarragon. Beat the eggs lightly with the single cream. Heat the butter in a 20 cm/8 inch omelette pan until it starts to foam. Pour in the eggs. As soon as the under part begins to set, spread the shrimp and cream mixture over the omelette. Lower the heat slightly and cook until the omelette is set all over but still moist. Fold the edges over towards the centre and slide on to a heated serving platter. Serve at once.

Terrinée de gigot à l'ancienne

BROILED LEG OF LAMB

WITH HARICOT BEANS

This ancient Normandy recipe was made with the Normandy *pré-salé* lamb from the Cotentin salt marshes, but the same result can be achieved with any fresh home-produced lamb.

◇

225 g/8 oz fresh or dried haricot beans, shelled
1 bouquet garni
salt and pepper
1 medium leg of lamb, boned
1 garlic clove
100 g/4 oz belly of pork, minced
225 g/8 oz small pickling onions or large spring onions
500 g/1 lb new potatoes, peeled
home-made chicken stock

SERVES 6

If using dried beans, soak them for 3 hours. Cook the beans for 1 hour in water with the bouquet garni, adding salt towards the end of the cooking time.

Season the lamb on both sides with salt and plenty of black pepper. Divide the garlic into fine slivers and stud the inside of the meat with it. Using butcher's string, tie the meat securely into a ball shape.

Preheat the oven to 190°C/375°F/gas mark 5. Place the minced pork in a large cast iron or earthenware casserole. Place the lamb in the centre. Cover and cook in the preheated oven for 30 minutes. Lower the oven heat to 150°C/300°F/gas mark 2. Take the lamb out and discard some of the fat, leaving enough to lubricate the sauce.

Drain the haricot beans. Replace the lamb in the centre of the dish, surrounded by the onions, then the beans and finally the potatoes. Season and cover with the chicken stock if necessary although there should not really be a sauce, just a nice moist coating around meat and vegetables. Cover the casserole and cook for 1 further hour or until meat and vegetables are tender. Serve the meat very hot, carved into thick slices, with the vegetables and minced pork moistened with the cooking juices.

Aspic de pommes au Calvados

APPLE ASPIC WITH CALVADOS

A very refreshing dessert to be served with *crème fraîche*. Use perfumed apples such as Cox's or Reinettes.

◇

500 g/1 lb sugar
75 ml/3 fl oz water
1 kg/2 lb apples, peeled and sliced
1 teaspoon Calvados
75 g/3 oz shredded almonds
a little sunflower oil

SERVES 6

Cook the sugar with the water in a large saucepan until syrupy. Add the sliced apples and the Calvados. Simmer over very low heat for 45 minutes, stirring well, so that it does not stick to the bottom of the pan.

Toast the almonds in a frying pan until golden but not browned. Add them to the apples. Lightly oil a 1 litre/1¾ pint aspic mould or soufflé dish. Spoon the apples into the dish. Tap the base of the dish on a work surface so that it packs well. Allow to cool, then cover and leave in the refrigerator for 24 hours until set. Serve chilled.

Pré-salé lamb or home-smoked herring or will be grilled in the kitchen fireplace.

— *La Collation Soupante* —

One Sunday afternoon I drove through the enchanting valley of the Risle river. A gracious meandering tributary of the Seine, it runs through pastoral watermeadows where brown-and-white cows drink at its banks, and through villages where it either graces the elegant gardens of half-timbered manor houses or lets itself be teased momentarily by an ancient water wheel. I was on my way to St-Grégoire-de-Vièvre where an old couple expected me for *la collation soupante*, a customary late afternoon Sunday meal in many rural communities of Normandy.

I have happy childhood memories of time spent with my parents at their friends' *chaumière*. I approached the gravel drive with nostalgia. The same freshly laundered needlepoint curtains hung at the latticed windows, the same wooden gate opened through a manicured box hedge, and inside were my parents' friends, now much older, in their calicoed Sunday best.

The décor had not changed, either. An antique carved dresser, *le vaissellier*, laden with old crockery, shining copper and pewter pots, the monotonous sound of the grandfather clock's pendulum and

among whimsical holiday souvenirs, yellowed family portraits and the toothy grins of the latest grandchildren.

First we had a cup of coffee and as the clock chimed five, Louis brought in from the cellar bottles of *cidre bouché*, the fizzy corked cider drunk on Sundays and special occasions, as opposed to flat cider which is drunk daily. As a first course Nénette put on the table a golden terrine of home made *rillettes de lapin*, potted rabbit. We ate it with slices of crusty *pain de campagne*, home-pickled gherkins and tiny onions. To follow, something I had not had in years – the real Normandy batavia lettuce, a firm, indigenous Webb, tossed in a dressing of chives, *crème fraîche* and cider vinegar.

We finished this early evening feast with luke-warm *bourdelots*, small pears poached first in a syrup flavoured with cloves and raspberry vinegar then wrapped and baked inside the finest of pastries. With these, a cold caramelized apple mould served with a home-made *crème anglaise*, the two desserts Nénette remembered I had liked so much as a child.

Rillettes de lapin

COARSE-CUT RABBIT PÂTÉ

1 large rabbit
1 kg/2 lb boned pork rib
750 g/1½ lb fatty belly of pork, rind removed
75 ml/3 fl oz white wine
50 ml/2 fl oz water
salt and pepper
2 shallots, chopped as finely as possible
a sprinkling of fresh thyme leaves.

SERVES 6

Cut the meat from the rabbit into cubes. Cut the pork and pork belly the same way. Pour the wine and water into a large cast iron or flameproof casserole. Put the mixed meats into the casserole pot with seasoning, and add the shallots and thyme. Cover and simmer over the lowest possible heat for 2½ hours, scraping the bottom of the dish with a wooden spoon from time to time so that the meat does not stick.

When all the meats are so tender that they are falling apart, shred them between two forks until a coarse paste is obtained. Check the seasoning and transfer to glass or earthenware preserving jars. Leave to cool, cover and keep in a cold room or refrigerator. Leave for at least 2 days before serving chilled. The *rillettes* will keep for 2–3 weeks if refrigerated.

Laitue Normande

NORMANDY SALAD DRESSING

FOR LETTUCE

The dressing must be kept cold or refrigerated until the lettuce is ready to be tossed. The charm of this dish is its freshness to the palate.

◇

1 tablespoon cider vinegar
75 ml/3 fl oz *crème fraîche*
2 teaspoons fresh chopped chives
salt and pepper

Make the dressing by mixing the cider vinegar with the *crème fraîche* and chives. Add seasoning to taste.

Rillettes de lapin – a recipe from a well-thumbed family scrapbook.

Crème caramel aux pommes

CARAMELIZED APPLE MOULD

750 g/1½ lb cooking apples, just ripe
1 vanilla pod
½ teaspoon finely grated lemon rind
100 g/4 oz caster sugar
50 g/2 oz unsalted butter, very soft
2 teaspoons plain flour
3 large eggs, beaten

CARAMEL
75 g/3 oz sugar
2 tablespoons water

SERVES 6

Preheat the oven to 190°C/375°F/gas mark 5.

Peel, core and slice the apples. Cook them gently to a purée with the vanilla pod, lemon rind and sugar. Leave to cool a little. Discard the vanilla pod. Transfer the apple purée to a mixing bowl. Work in the butter, then the flour, and finally the beaten eggs.

To make the caramel, put the sugar and water into a small pan. Cook over moderate heat, stirring constantly until the caramel is a rich brown. Pour into a 1 litre/1¾ pint soufflé dish and turn well around so that the bottom and sides are covered.

Spoon the apple mixture into the dish. Stand in a pan of warm water and bake in the preheated oven for 40–45 minutes until set and the blade of a knife inserted at the centre comes out clean. Cool at room temperature and refrigerate overnight, before serving.

Crème anglaise

-------- HOME-MADE CUSTARD --------

This sauce is so delicious served cold with many desserts that it is well worth sparing the time to prepare it.

◇

450 ml/¾ pint milk
1 vanilla pod
5 egg yolks
6 tablespoons caster sugar
a pinch of salt

-------- SERVES 4–6 --------

Scald the milk with the vanilla pod slit in half. Leave to infuse for a few minutes, then discard the pod.

In a mixing bowl, work the egg yolks, sugar and salt together until pale and frothy. Work in the milk, a little at a time.

Transfer to a heavy-based saucepan and thicken the sauce over the lowest possible heat, stirring constantly. The sauce is ready when it coats the back of a spoon well. Leave to cool at room temperature. Refrigerate for at least 2 hours before serving.

Les bourdelots

-------- POACHED PEARS IN A PASTRY CASE --------

6 small firm pears
750 g/1½ lb puff pastry
2 tablespoons sugar
25 g/1 oz unsalted butter

SYRUP
150 g/5 oz sugar
125 ml/4 fl oz water
1 clove
2 teaspoons raspberry vinegar

GLAZE
1 egg yolk mixed with a little water

-------- SERVES 6 --------

Peel the pears, leaving them whole with the stems on. Using a corer, core each pear from the base. In a pan make the syrup by bringing to the boil the sugar, water, clove and raspberry vinegar. Poach the pears in the syrup until they feel half-cooked. Leave to cool in the syrup for 6 hours, turning them once.

Preheat the oven to 200°C/400°F/gas mark 6.

Roll out the pastry and divide into 6 squares each large enough to wrap a whole fruit. Pat each pear dry with kitchen paper and place at the centre of each square. Fold the pastry edges towards the stem, giving a twist to secure. Seal all the edges by running a wet pastry brush on each side of the pastry, then pressing together. Glaze with the egg and water mixture. Bake in the preheated oven until the pastry is cooked and golden brown. Serve the pears lukewarm on their own or with *crème fraîche*.

— CHAPTER 3 —

Brittany

Make your way to any cove on the Brittany coast and you have the sea for breakfast, lunch and dinner. You have only to watch the treacherous sea battling against the rocks to guess the freshness of the catch. Lobster, crab, mussels and all types of fish abound. Drive inland and you enter the solid culinary traditions of the *Bretagne bretonnante*.

This buttress of a headland distinctly detached from the mass of the French continent is a constant ethnic and geographic divide. There is the ArMor, the long coastline jagged to the north by the force of France's most vengeful seas, while the south coast has a myriad sandy shores and flowery islands bathed by the Gulf Stream. Inland is the ArGoat, a wild, untamed landscape of moorlands, forests, lakes and rolling hills which the Bretons like to regard as their 'mountains'. Everywhere, as if to unite this land of infinite contrasts, the same slated grey roofs and dormer windows of the typical Breton houses, judiciously protected by the gentle camber of the landscape – between the gorse and the druidic stones they emerge like indigenous toadstools.

The ethnic divide is more complex – a mixture of Celtic and Gaelic certainly but also *chouan* Cornouaillais, Tregorien, each attached to different traditions and even dialects, each of different stature, physiognomy and temperament. In addition, from early spring to the end of the summer months there is the French tourist who invades the region. He rushes to Brittany to feel the sting of the salt on his lips, to capture dramatic sunsets from some wild coastal point, to retrace the steps of the ancient Celts or simply – and mostly – to enjoy the freshest of seafood or the crispest of pancakes. For

together with the mounds of crustaceans consumed as *plateaux de fruits de mer*, *crêpes* and buckwheat *galettes* must be the main culinary symbol of Brittany.

If in other parts of France pseudo-*crêperies bretonnes* have opened where *crêpes* are kiwied, mangoed or extravagantly flambéed, in Brittany at least they are still served traditionally – most of all in the Breton home.

The pancake was part of the staple Breton diet before bread even figured on the daily table. Often made on large griddles in a special outbuilding (*la crêperie*), the pancakes are prepared in great piles by the Breton housewife on Fridays and will be cut cold during the week for breakfast, and to accompany soups, *lait ribot* – the local buttermilk – or stewed fruit. If cooked at the last minute to be eaten hot, the buckwheat *galette* will be filled with a soft egg, a local sausage or thin slices of *andouille*, the Breton chitterling speciality.

Until not long ago, the pig was the mainstay of the Breton family and it is held that if asked whether he preferred his wife or his children, the *paysan Breton* would answer, 'my pig'. Today, *charcuterie de Bretagne* has a great reputation all over France and if *andouille* and *andouillette* are for attuned palates only, the coarse garlicky pâté rarely fails to please. Ham and salt pork are used in

Fishing boats at Le Conquet, Brittany.

many recipes such as *potée*, to which a handful of freshly podded haricot beans is added, as in another well-known dish, *gigot à la bretonne*, lamb roasted and served with a mixture of the same beans and tomatoes.

Brittany is also the land of *primeurs*, young vegetables grown on iodinized soil, such as tender new potatoes, *petits pois*, tiny carrots and green beans. And, of course, it would be impossible to forget the plump artichokes from Roscoff, or the cauliflowers, or the massive yield of onions and shallots. As well as being used at home or sent to the markets of Europe, these vegetables find their way to the canning plants of the region, supplementing the speciality tinned sardines of Concarneau.

At home, simple food is prepared. In search of native recipes, I spent some time in the kitchens of a fisherman's wife on the Côtes du Nord and a farmer's wife from the ArGoat. More than anywhere else I found folk still very attached to the way of life of their ancestors, in their homes and in their lifestyle generally. With some notable exceptions, the Breton cuisine is a no-nonsense affair.

The Sea for Breakfast, Lunch and Dinner

On my way to the salty shores of St-Jacut-de-la-mer, on the picturesque northern coast of Brittany, I lunched with a friend in her adoptive village of Miniac Morvan. Although she is a Parisian, she bought her house there some twenty years ago and delights in the preparation of *les produits de la mer*.

She gave me succulent *praires farcies*, large clams bubbling hot from the oven filled with the finest of garlic mixtures. To follow, we shared a laudable tart made with fresh scallops and an unusual pastry. With it the wine of Southern Brittany, the most northerly in the west, a Muscadet.

As I left I felt drawn to visit nearby Dinan, a favourite place of mine I had not seen in years. What a disappointment! The sleepy ancient port of the languid Rance river is now totally given over to the fantasy and paraphernalia of tourist attraction. The river banks, once wild, are jewelled with fibre-glass yachts, the small riverside Routier restaurant, where I had my first taste of the Breton shellfish *ormeau*, and a memorable veal escalope cooked with *fruits de mer* by a jolly *patronne*, is now yet another twee canopied restaurant. A lone working farm remains on the opposite bank of the river looking almost out of place amidst such an over-dressed utopia.

However, by the time I reached the little fishing port of St-Jacut, a small peninsula festooned with coves and sandy beaches, I had quite forgotten the disappointment of Dinan. I had driven through country lanes so disused that the grass grows in the centre of the road, passed fields where small handmade haystacks were carefully packed under the arches of gnarled cider apple trees. In St-Jacut I was the guest of a fisherman's family. In the small backyard among white lilies and masses of pink and blue hydrangeas, fishing nets were spread out to dry on an ancient fishing boat. Cackling gulls fed by the kitchen door, the air was pure ozone. Inside the long stone cottage, I found the practical comfort of people who do not spend much time indoors. Father, mother and son are involved daily with their fishing and retailing business.

For dinner we had the speciality of the Brittany coast, *la cotriade*. I was very curious to see how it would be served as the recipe varies according to the part of Brittany one is in. Known as the *pot-au-feu des pêcheurs* – fisherman's stew – it is a wholesome dish of various kinds of fish cooked with leeks and potatoes. We ate the stock first, poured into individual soup bowls over large slices of *pain de campagne*. Then we had the fish, potatoes and leeks with a peppery vinaigrette dressing and more bread. The fish had been caught that day, the potatoes and leeks dug from the garden. Everything tasted so fresh, it was a delight and a welcome change from the puréed red fish soup and garlic mayonnaise which should only belong to the South but is unfortunately served all over France these days.

Everyone had gone well before I woke up the following morning, but Maryvonne had left me a breakfast of rye and seaweed bread, a new speciality of the Breton bakers. I ate it with lashings of butter which had been hand-laced with sea salt.

Late evening in Ouessant.

Praires farcies

CLAMS WITH GARLIC BUTTER

24 *praires* (fresh clams)
50 g/2 oz fine fresh breadcrumbs
2 garlic cloves
50 g/2 oz butter
50 g/2 oz *crème fraîche*
2 tablespoons finely chopped parsley
salt and pepper

SERVES 4

Preheat the oven to its hottest setting. Wash and brush the *praires*. Place the breadcrumbs in a mixing bowl. Open the *praires* over the bowl by inserting the sharp blade of a strong knife near the shell hinge and turning it. Let the liquid drain over the breadcrumbs.

Discard the upper shells and place the *praires* in their lower shells in a large baking dish. Crush the garlic as finely as possible and pound it together with the breadcrumbs and all the other ingredients. Spoon some of the mixture into each shell. Place in the very hot oven for 5 minutes. Serve at once with crusty bread.

Tarte aux coquilles St-Jacques

SCALLOP TART

PASTRY
125 ml/4 fl oz dry white wine
100 g/4 oz salted butter
225 g/8 oz plain white flour

FILLING
12 scallops, prepared
50 g/2 oz butter
4 eggs
250 ml/8 fl oz *crème fraîche*
2 teaspoons tomato purée
a pinch of saffron
salt and pepper

SERVES 6

Have your fishmonger prepare the scallops out of their shell leaving only the round white meat and the crescent-shaped 'coral'.

Make the pastry 2 hours in advance. Warm the wine in a saucepan until lukewarm. Add the butter a small piece at a time, using a hand whisk, until the mixture is creamy. Remove from the heat and add the sifted flour spoon by spoon, mixing well all the time until the dough, which will be very sticky at first, forms a ball and detaches itself from the pan. Leave to rest in a cool place for 2 hours.

Preheat the oven to 200°C/400°F/gas mark 6. Coarsely chop the white scallop meats, reserving the coral. Sauté the scallop meat in butter for a few seconds. Beat the eggs with the *crème fraîche* and add the tomato purée, saffron, salt and pepper.

Roll out the pastry and use to line a 30 cm/12 inch tart dish. Arrange the scallop meat and coral in a pattern over the pastry. Pour the creamy mixture on to the shellfish. Bake in the preheated oven for 30–35 minutes or until the filling is set and golden-brown. Serve at once or while still warm.

Gatherings from a walk on the beach.

La cotriade des pêcheurs

FISHERMAN'S STEW

Any cold-water fish may be used, such as whiting or other white fish, mackerel, conger eel, even one or two fresh sardines (only if you like a strong tasting stock).

◇

1.5 kg/3 lb mixed fish
1 tablespoon sunflower oil
2 onions, chopped
1 kg/2 lb medium new potatoes
salt and pepper
water
1 glass white wine
a few parsley and chervil sprigs
fresh thyme and bayleaf
1 garlic clove
6 leeks

VINAIGRETTE SAUCE
2 tablespoons white wine vinegar or cider vinegar
6 tablespoons sunflower oil
a few fresh tarragon leaves, finely chopped

SERVES 6

Clean the fish. Discard the heads, tails and fins and cut the fish into largish chunks. Heat the oil in a large pot and sauté the onions until transparent. Add the potatoes, quartered, salt and pepper, and cover with water and the white wine. Tie together the parsley, chervil, thyme and bayleaf and add to the pot with the garlic. Cover and cook until the potatoes are half cooked.

Now add the leeks and the larger pieces of fish. Bring to the boil, adding a little more water if necessary so that you are left with enough stock. Cook over high heat for 15 minutes, then add the smaller fish and cook for a further 5 minutes. The fish should be just cooked but not falling to pieces or coming off the bones.

To serve: carefully scoop the fish, leeks and potatoes out of the stock, cover with a little stock and keep warm. Discard the garlic and bouquet garni. Pour the rest of the stock into a soup tureen in which slices of bread have been placed. Eat the soup first, then the fish and vegetables with the vinaigrette, made by whisking all the ingredients together, and crusty bread.

The sea for dinner – la cotriade des pêcheurs

—— Lunch with Mam-Goz ——

Despite the bright July sunshine left behind in the Côtes du Nord I made my way to the farm set on the lonely moors of the Parc Régional d'Armorique in thick fog rolling off the sea. It was hot and clammy.

As I drew to a halt in the farmyard, I was met at once by four generations of the Leguen family. It was Sunday and Mam-Goz (grand-mère) Leguen was wearing the black frock and neatly ironed white coif of the region, an outfit she would wear for Sunday mass and special occasions until her last day. Within seconds of my arrival a large refreshing glass of *pétillant* Brittany cider was pressed into my hand and we all drank to each other's *Yerc'hed-Mad* – good health. Anne Leguen had been one of my teachers in my youth and this was the first time I had visited her since she married a farmer and returned to her native land; now she was a grandmother.

And so, to the dining room for *un déjeuner campagnard*. The table had been laid with *grand-mère's* old Quimper dinner service, a collection of off-white and blue china with brightly coloured flowers and Breton figurines in their national costumes painted at the centre of each plate. The cider which was to accompany the meal was served not in glasses but in *bolées* (small china bowls). Around the room stood heavily carved dark oak furniture, a crucifix and other religious artifacts reminding one of the strong Catholic culture of the region. The divider between the dining room and the large kitchen where lunch simmered on an Aga stove bought at a country fair fifty years ago was a piece of furniture I thought was really just a thing of the past, but apparently it still figures in country homes. This was the famous *lit clos*, a bed set in a lattice-work of oak with doors and curtains for privacy, in which people would sleep in the main room, in order to keep warm.

Our Sunday lunch was brought to the table. It was *Kig-Ha-Farz*, a rustic single dish of three types of meat simmered for hours with potatoes and various vegetables. With it, the *Farz*, a dumpling of buckwheat, prunes and raisins cooked in the stock inside a cloth (*farz sa'ch*) and served with the meat in thick slices. For dessert we ate *crêpes de Mam-Goz*, wafer-thin moist pancakes made with grated apples macerated in the local apple *eau-de-vie*, Lambig. The recipes were all very foreign to me and the sweet dumpling eaten with the meat reminded me of the more northerly links between the Bretons and their British Celtic cousins.

Lunch was jolly. Grand-mère and grandchildren were so pleased to have the excuse of a traditional meal to recall the past. I heard about the day they still kill the pig and all the recipes were described in full detail. They recalled the old Breton weddings which lasted a week and to which thousands of people were invited. At this point, Jean Leguen put on a record of regional bagpipe and accordion music. Mam-Goz, who had had quite a lot of cider, was pink-cheeked and giggly by now. She sat by me and started telling me about her own parents' wedding. 'I was five when my parents got married and I remember the piper getting drunk and the bagpipe falling all the way down the hill,' she said . . . I just listened, pleased for all of them that holy matrimony had managed to produce such a lovely family over the years.

Opposite: A typical griddle for home-made Breton pancakes.

Kig-Ha-Farz

—————— BRETON MEAT STEW WITH ——————
BUCKWHEAT DUMPLING

MEAT POT AU FEU
1 kg/2 lb beef (top rump) in one piece
1 kg/2 lb salt-cured ham
10 carrots
10 turnips
4 swedes
10 leeks
6 onions (one studded with 2 cloves)
4 shallots
1 bouquet garni
pepper
5 litres/9 pints water
1 hearty cabbage
2 large smoked garlic sausages

DUMPLING
500 g/1 lb buckwheat flour
1 teaspoon salt
4 eggs
25 g/1 oz butter, softened
25 g/1 oz lard, softened
2 tablespoons caster sugar
a large pinch of black pepper
150 ml/5 fl oz milk
water
100 g/4 oz raisins
100 g/4 oz prunes, stoned and coarsely chopped

—————— SERVES 10 ——————

Wash and peel the vegetables, and leave them whole. Place all the ingredients except the cabbage and the sausages in a large pot. Bring to the boil, skim the surface carefully and lower the heat. Simmer for 2 hours.

Meanwhile, make the dumpling. Sift the flour and salt into a large mixing bowl. Make a well in the centre. Add the eggs, the butter and lard softened at room temperature, the sugar and black pepper. Mix well with a wooden spatula, then slowly add the milk and enough water until a very thick batter is obtained. Then add the raisins and prunes. Leave to rest for 1 hour.

Onions are a staple of traditional Breton recipes.

If you do not have a dumpling bag, it is not too difficult to make one. Spoon the mixture into the centre of a strong linen cloth, such as a tea-towel, fold the corners towards the centre and tie securely with string. Add the dumpling to the *pot au feu* and continue simmering for a further 2 hours.

Forty-five minutes before serving, add the cabbage, quartered, and the garlic sausages, having pricked the skin carefully. To serve, arrange the sliced meat and dumpling on a flat heated platter. Serve the vegetables and broth in a large dish and eat all together, spooning over enough broth to moisten the meat.

Les crêpes de Mam-Goz

—————— AUTHENTIC BRETON PANCAKES ——————

Although they were made by Anne on the griddle I would suggest cooking these in a large frying pan, making sure that they are as thin as possible. Pour just enough mixture into the greased heated pan and spread quickly over the bottom, tilting the pan and adding a little more mixture if necessary.

The apples must cook as quickly as the pancake, so they will need to be grated finely and sprinkled with a little sugar and *eau-de-vie*.

◇

500 g/1 lb plain white flour
6 eggs
25 g/1 oz slightly salted butter, melted
½ teaspoon finely grated lemon rind
milk
6 medium dessert apples such as Cox's
or any perfumed variety
a dash of *eau-de-vie* (Calvados or other fruit)
vanilla sugar

—————— MAKES AT LEAST 12 ——————

Sift the flour into a mixing bowl. Make a well in the centre and break in the eggs, add the melted butter, lemon rind and a little milk. Work the eggs into the flour with a wooden spatula, adding more milk and water if necessary until the right consistency is obtained. Grate the apples finely and mix with the *eau-de-vie* and a little sugar. Mix the apple with the pancake batter. Cook the pancakes immediately in a greased pancake pan. Serve at once with a sprinkling of vanilla sugar.

—— The Isle of Ouessant ——

One hot July morning I stepped on to a fishing boat at the cobbled port of Le Conquet, near Brest, leaving behind the rediscovered traditions of mainland Brittany, ready to capture at source the legendary arcane life of the isolated islanders of Ouessant.

I wanted to see for myself the way of life of fewer than 600 people who are cut off from the mainland by bad weather for three-quarters of the year, whose men spend most of their time at sea, whose women work the land and tend the sheep and have always played such an important role in

the daily life of the island that they are allowed the privilege of proposing marriage.

On the way we stopped at the small island of Molene to collect fish and crustaceans. From the boat one could see the dramatic coastline of the mainland behind, the land's end of France, its grey granite gnarled by the elements into claws which grasp at the ocean.

On Ouessant, the sheep grazing among sun-kissed gorse and an expanse of heather, the azure painted shutters on the whitewashed cottages, the graceful glide of the gulls caught in the summer

thermals or the quick trill of the oystercatchers as they flew by, made it difficult to understand the harsh life my fishing companion was describing as we walked towards the island's small town – Lampaul. But when his ageing grandmother opened her cottage door to greet us, her large frame and wizened face under the austere black coif and costume, her feet in cloglike black shoes, her deeply chapped hands, her sad steel-grey eyes which had long forgotten to smile, explained it all.

question I was intruding on the privacy of her thoughts about her past and present life. She could not understand how so much hardship could be described with glamour by her grandchild. Most of the time she waved dismissively, poking the grate where the *ragoût à la motte* was simmering.

I was intrigued by this unaccustomed way of cooking. She explained. While the men were at sea and the women worked the land this cooking method ensured that a hot stew and a hot dessert

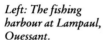

Left: The fishing harbour at Lampaul, Ouessant.

The house with blue shutters at Ouessant.

Inside, the cottage was simply kept. Every piece of wood or crockery or even linen was either white or blue like the shutters outside. 'They are the colours of the Virgin Mary', said the old lady, crossing herself while pointing at a tapestry of Mother and Child over the mantelshelf.

Without uttering another word, she moved slowly towards a cupboard and poured us some milk which we drank while eating a piece of home-made buttery *gâteau breton*. As we sat there, I studied the difference between the young and the old. The grandson who was so keen to explain their way of life – the poor soil, how they collect the top of the peat for cooking the traditional lamb stew, how they tag the ears of sheep so that each family recognizes its own, the perilous fishing expeditions. He was full of the enthusiasm of youth and pride in his ancestral heritage. On the other hand the grandmother was reserved and undemonstrative. I felt that with each

would be ready without having to be watched when the family returned home in the evening. Today this *ragoût* is still the traditional dish of Ouessant. The stew is started first on the stove in a large cast-iron pot, which is placed inside the fireplace on a bed of thinly cut turf from the peat fields. More turf is arranged around the pot until it is totally buried. The turf is then lighted and soon, like a pipe, combusts for three to four hours, keeping the stew at the same simmering temperature all the way through. Often another mound of turf is prepared with a *Farz*, the Breton dessert, simmering inside. Both the meat and dessert I tasted were succulent, especially as the lamb was the *pré salé* type, grazed on the salt-laden grass of the Ouessant cliffs. Both had a slightly smoky taste. Just in case you can find turf from the peat fields, the recipe is given. The less intrepid will be relieved to hear that it is possible to use a conventional oven for this delicious Breton speciality.

Ragout d'agneau à la motte

—— LAMB STEW, COOKED IN TURF ——

Cheaper cuts of lamb such as middle end of neck cutlets may be used for this recipe.

◇

25 g/1 oz lard
1 kg/2 lb onions, sliced
1 kg/2 lb lamb
500 g/1 lb carrots, sliced
1 kg/2 lb potatoes, peeled
salt and pepper
a pinch of thyme
2 bayleaves
water

—— SERVES 6 ——

Heat the lard in a large cast iron pot. Sauté the onions until just golden but not browned and set aside, then sauté the lamb on all sides until brown. Return the onions to the pot and add the carrots, the potatoes and seasoning. Bury the thyme and bayleaves in the centre. Cover with lukewarm water and place inside turf as described in the text. The same dish may also be cooked for 4 hours in a very low oven.

Far d'Ouessant aux pruneaux

—— PRUNE AND BACON FLAN ——

Although a dessert, a few small *lardons* are found in this dish – another reflection of the customary Breton way of mixing sweet and savoury.

◇

100 g/4 oz plain flour
100 g/4 oz sugar
2 eggs
600 ml/1 pint milk
75 g/3 oz very small cubes of smoked ham
100 g/4 oz prunes, stoned and
soaked in 1 tablespoon rum or *eau-de-vie*
butter

—— SERVES 4–6 ——

Preheat the oven to 160°C/325°F/gas mark 3.

Sift the flour and sugar into a mixing bowl, add the eggs and work into the flour, adding the milk gradually. Generously butter an earthenware baking dish. Mix the lardons and chopped prunes in the bottom of the dish. Pour the mixture into the dish and bake in the preheated oven for 50–60 minutes or until the surface feels set to the touch or the blade of a knife comes out clean. Serve lukewarm or cold.

A china cupboard on Ouessant – (with kind permission of the Ecomuseum).

Gâteau breton

—— HOME-MADE BRETON CAKE ——

100 g/4 oz plain flour
25 g/1 oz salted butter
100 g/4 oz caster sugar
2 teaspoons dark rum
3 egg yolks
milk, to glaze

—— SERVES 4–6 ——

Preheat the oven to 160°C/325°F/gas mark 3.

Sift the flour into a mixing bowl and make a well in the centre. Cut the butter, which should not be too firm, into small pieces and place in the well together with the sugar, rum and egg yolks. Work well together with a fork or your fingertips until a sticky mixture is obtained.

Gâteau breton.

Generously butter a round 20 cm/8 inch cake tin, then sprinkle a little flour all over the surface to prevent the cake from sticking. Spoon the mixture into the cake tin. Make a criss-cross design on the surface with a knife, glaze with a little milk and bake in the preheated oven for 45 minutes or until the cake is golden brown, firm to the touch and comes away from the sides of the tin slightly.

Leave to cool in the tin for a few minutes, then turn on to a wire rack and leave to cool completely. Serve cold, as an afternoon cake.

— CHAPTER 4 —

The West

VENDÉE · POITOU
CHARENTE-MARITIME · SAINTONGE

I left Brittany to rediscover the Pays d'Ouest, a region which faces the Atlantic from Vendée to the Gironde and whose frontiers inland extend as far as the Limousin.

Historically the region is famous for its savage religious wars, with strongholds such as La Rochelle and Poitiers. Geographically it is the route between Paris and Aquitaine. Very little is spoken about its natural culinary attractions, the character of its people or indeed the great charm of its inland sleepy flatness and some of its coastline.

If most of the coast of Vendée has been spoilt by property developers who have been allowed to eradicate centuries of France's natural habitat and dot the shores with characterless concrete holiday homes, at least further down the coast or on the picturesque islands of Yeu, Ré and Oléron the authenticity of the original landscape is still there. And then there is the verdant Marais Poitevin, a stunning maze of waterways along the Sèvre-Niortaise where the colours of the earth and water blend. Further down lie the sunflower fields and vineyards of Saintonge and Cognac itself.

The origins of the people of the Pays d'Ouest are diverse: Celts in Vendée – but also descendants of the Dutch who came to tend the marshland – and Iberians from the south. However, all speak the same dialect originated from the *langue d'oïl*, which was the official language of Northern France in the sixteenth century. The language of the South was then the *langue d'oc* and both are now only reflected in a few everyday expressions and culinary terms: haricot beans are called *mojettes* or *monjettes*; snails, *lumas* or *cagouilles*;

The sunflower fields of the Pays d'Ouest.

geese not *oies*, as in the rest of France, but *oches*.

The local products are good. For a start, the butter, *beurre des Charentes*, is renowned as the finest in France. Fish from the Atlantic is always fresh and succulent: a speciality of the region is the little flat fish, *céteau*, a tiny delicate sole, served fried or *meunière*. *La chaudrée*, the local fish stew is very similar to the Breton *cotriade*. In the Baie de l'Aiguillon, between Vendée and the Charente-Maritime, large mussels grow on stakes and one man alone can harvest up to three tons a day. Many local *mouclades*, spiced mussel dishes as popular in the region as *moules à la marinière*, will be made with this mollusc. Around Marennes, facing the Ile d'Oléron, there is a massive stretch of oyster beds. The oysters are eaten *nature* or with a *tartine de grattons*, a kind of rillette spread on bread, and also with pâté.

The excellent ducks of Vendée are reared on the Marais of Challans and sold on market day in large double baskets, their heads peeping out of each flap. Geese are also a speciality and as a precursor to the neighbouring recipes of Dordogne and Gascony, a *compote* of goose is prepared in the Poitou. Guinea fowl and rabbit are braised with cabbage; the original recipe for hare, *lièvre à la Royale*, is a culinary *tour de force* and takes days to prepare.

Vegetables figures at most meals. There is, of course, the orange-fleshed sweet Charentais melon which is eaten as a first course drenched with the local Pineau des Charentes, a drink made of Cognac added to freshly pressed grape juice. Broad beans, *fèves*, are either puréed with butter, parsley and garlic or served as a soup. Cabbage is quickly boiled then mashed with a fork with butter, salt and plenty of black pepper. It is then called *l'embeurrée*. Leeks, sometimes found wild in the vineyards of Saintonge, are cut young and served like asparagus with melted butter or a vinaigrette sauce. Green and haricot beans are either eaten cold in salads or sautéed in butter and garlic with baby carrots. In Vendée, the white haricot beans are baked with carrots and herbs in an earthenware pot. Butter and thick cream are added just before serving.

For desserts wild angelica is used a great deal and there are deliciously light preparations with milk, not dissimilar to junket, which are served with a sprinkling of sugar and Cognac.

The Marais Poitevin and an
—— Evening with a Cook in Romanesque Vendée ——

I nearly gave up my foray to the Venise Verte, the green Venice of the Marais Poitevin. I am so pleased I didn't – I spent an afternoon in a haven of peace, drank fragrant wine, ate delicious food and met a professional cook who gave me lots of tips on the local cuisine.

One baking July morning, still deeply disappointed by the newly built Vendée coast and a night spent on the drab sea-front at Les Sables d'Olonne, I pointed my car towards the Marais Poitevin and drove for what seemed hours through parched fields, mosquito-infested fens and dunes, a landscape cheered only from place to place by fields of sunflowers. I was about to turn back when I noticed the green line along the Sèvre Niortaise on my map. According to Michelin, a green line is supposed to mean a place of exceptional natural beauty – in fact it usually means that trees grow there, as I have found to my cost on many of my journeys through France. I nonetheless decided to battle on to the town of Niort.

Suddenly, as I followed the course of the river, desiccated austerity gave way to vivid greenery. Small fields and waterways were bordered by copses of poplars and beech trees, banks filled with wild angelica, scented mint and feathery meadow-sweet. Dotted along the towpaths stood simple long white-washed houses, *les cabanes*, with a punt moored by each one, and here and there a large black umbrella sheltering a lone fisherman from the scorching sun, or a punt slowly going by with a calf or a few goats on board. For the waterways are the only way the *maraichin* can travel from field to field. Daily life ticks over, as if detached from the rest of the world. Only when the mean westerly wind blows straight from the nearby ocean is it time to hustle.

Those were my thoughts about the area as I sat at a small café-auberge enjoying every mouthful of a *friture d'anguilles*, a dish of eels deep-fried with a few coarsely cut potatoes and served with a generous covering of chopped garlic and parsley. Exquisitely simple, I could not have wished for a better midday snack. With it, an iced *pichet* of crisp, young white Vin des Charentes. To finish and clear the palate, a mild, creamy local goat's milk cheese.

I left mid-afternoon to go and stay with friends who have a Renaissance *fief*, not far from the Romanesque church of Vouvant. The ancient house is amazing, built of stone around a completely enclosed garden. In the flag-stoned kitchen, with its stone sink, cast iron cooker, and seventeenth-century meatsafe, I met Huguette, their cook. She originates from the region and is a mine of information on local food and dishes. For our dinner served in an imposing room flanked by a monumental fireplace she had prepared some *coeurs de laitue poitevins*, firm lettuce hearts served with melted butter, salt, pepper and finely crushed garlic; as a main course, a fricassee of white tuna with *mojettes*, and for dessert a *tourteau fromage*, a baked cheesecake made with the local goat's milk cheese, well risen with a thick black crust. She also gave me two interesting recipes for *escargots* which I shall pass on.

The Marais Poitevin: 'Dotted along the towpath – simple long white-washed houses'.

Fricassée de thon blanc

—— FRESH TUNA FRICASSEE ——

600 g/1¼ lb fresh white tuna
500 g/1 lb large ripe tomatoes
2 tablespoons olive oil
3 garlic cloves, chopped
3 fresh thyme sprigs
3 fresh bayleaves
salt and pepper
2 glasses very dry white wine
chopped parsley and crushed garlic, for the garnish

—— SERVES 4 ——

Skin and cube the fish. Run the tomatoes under hot water for a few seconds, then skin and coarsely chop them. Heat the oil in a cast iron or flameproof casserole and sauté the fish with the chopped garlic until golden but not browned. Add the tomatoes, then the thyme, bayleaves, salt, pepper and wine.

Simmer, covered for 30 minutes. Cook uncovered for a further 15 minutes, increasing the heat slightly, until the sauce is thick enough to coat the pieces of fish. Transfer to a heated serving dish and sprinkle with a mixture of chopped parsley and a tiny amount of finely crushed garlic. Check the seasoning; it should be quite peppery. Serve with *mojettes à la charentaise (recipe follows)*.

Les mojettes à la charentaise

—— HARICOT BEANS ——

1 kg/2 lb haricot beans in the pod
or 500 g/1 lb dried haricot beans
2 onions, one studded with a clove
1 garlic clove
1 large carrot
1 celery stick
1 bouquet garni
salt
butter

—— SERVES 6 ——

Pod the fresh beans or if using dried beans, soak them for 3 hours in lukewarm water. Drain well before cooking. Place the beans and all other ingredients except the salt and butter in a flame-

proof pot and cover with water. Bring to the boil, then cover and simmer slowly for 1 hour if fresh, or 1½ hours for dried, until the beans are tender but not mushy. Make sure the water does not evaporate – keep adding lukewarm water. Add salt only towards the end of cooking time or the beans will toughen.

To serve, drain the beans well and discard the onions, garlic, celery and bouquet garni. Chop the carrot coarsely, and mix it in a heated serving dish with the beans and a generous knob of butter. Check the seasoning.

Old-fashioned wooden meatsafe in Romanesque Vendée.

Opposite: Eel fishing in the Marais Poitevin.

Lumas à la chair à saucisse

EDIBLE SNAILS WITH
SAUSAGE-MEAT STUFFING

The *petits gris* variety of snail is needed for this recipe. Large *escargots de Bourgogne* would be less suitable. *Escargots* can now easily be found in tins, cooked in a *court-bouillon*. They are usually excellent; the shells can be purchased separately.

◇

6 dozen cooked *petits gris escargots*

FILLING
100 g/4 oz pork sausage-meat
2 garlic cloves, finely crushed
2 shallots, very finely chopped
1 heaped tablespoon finely chopped parsley
1 teaspoon finely chopped tarragon leaves
black pepper

SERVES 6

Preheat the oven to 230°C/450°F/gas mark 8.
In a mixing bowl mix all the filling ingredients together well. Spoon a little into each shell containing an *escargot*. Place in a large baking dish. Bake in the preheated oven for 15 minutes.

Lumas en sauce

ESCARGOTS BAKED IN A WINE SAUCE

Tinned *escargots* may be purchased at any good delicatessen. The tins specify the quantity in dozens. Tinned *escargots* are prepared in a spicy *court-bouillon* stock which should be kept for the preparation of this recipe.

◇

6 dozen cooked *petits gris escargots*

SAUCE
4 shallots
3 garlic cloves
1 knob butter
2 teaspoons plain flour
the *court-bouillon* from the tin
1 glass red wine
1 glass white wine
pepper
2 heaped tablespoons chopped parsley

SERVES 6

To make the sauce, chop the shallots and 2 garlic cloves as finely as possible. Heat the butter in a deep sauté pan and sauté the garlic and shallots until golden. Sprinkle the flour over the mixture, mix well and sauté for a little longer, then add the *court-bouillon*, the red wine and the white wine. Cover and let the sauce simmer for 15 minutes, adding some lukewarm water if the amount of liquid is not sufficient.

Preheat the oven to 230°C/450°F/gas mark 8. Place the *escargots* without their shells in 6 individual ramekins or baking dishes. Pour the sauce over them. Crush the remaining garlic clove and mix it with freshly ground black pepper and the parsley. Sprinkle over each dish. Bake in the preheated oven for 15 minutes. Serve with crusty bread.

Tourteau fromagé

BAKED CHEESECAKE

PASTRY
100 g/4 oz plain flour
50 g/2 oz unsalted butter
1 egg yolk
water

FILLING
90 g/3½ oz *fromage frais* (goat's or cow's milk)
50 g/2 oz caster sugar
50 g/2 oz plain flour
½ teaspoon baking powder
2 eggs

SERVES 6

First make the pastry and leave to rest for 1 hour. Roll out the dough and line a 20 cm/8 inch quiche dish with it.

For the filling, combine the cheese and sugar in a large bowl, then add the flour which has been sifted with the baking powder. Mix well. Separate the eggs and add the egg yolks to the cheese mixture one at a time, mixing constantly. Whisk the egg whites until stiff, then fold into the mixture. Pour into the pastry-lined dish and set aside in a cold room for 1 hour.

Preheat the oven to 200°C/400°F/gas mark 6. Bake the cheesecake for 40–45 minutes or until set and risen and the blade of a knife comes out clean when inserted into the centre.

Opposite: A baronial dining-room in the Vendée.

—— July 14th at the Oyster Farm ——

The French have a penchant for setting things on fire on July 14th. Last July at Chailerette, near Royan, Liliane and Elie Sala set fire to a pile of mussels, as they do at every *fête nationale*.

What they did, in fact, was to cook a gigantic *terrée*, otherwise known as an *éclade*, for their friends and relatives on the site of their oyster farm in the Marais de la Seudre. The *terrée* is an ancient tradition of the region – originally the simplest of ways for the fisherman to feed himself. He would gather a few mussels, pack them together in dried sea mud (hence the name *terrée*, meaning 'cooked on the earth'), then cover the shellfish with pine needles from the nearby forest and set fire to the needles. The heat would make the shellfish open

and cook into a smoky delicacy. These days, it is traditionally a dish for festivities and is done on a grander scale. A kind of barbecue of the sea, it is great fun, and the taste of the sweetly smoked mussels, eaten with black pepper and large slices of *pain de campagne*, buttered with the local *beurre des Charentes*, is quite an experience.

In true French style, while we were eating one dish we were talking of another one, and I learnt how the large Bouchot mussels are prepared quite differently in the region. Liliane cooks her *mouclade* with fresh basil and makes a splendid dish of *moules marinières* cooked with white wine, of course, but also with some vinegar, garlic, onion and basil again.

Above: an oyster shed in the Marais de la Seudre.

Opposite: At the oyster farm.

La terrée

MUSSELS BAKED IN PINE NEEDLES

A marvellous improvised barbecue.

◇

You will need:
1 large wooden plank
as many pine needles as possible to get a good fire
500 g/1 lb large Bouchot mussels per person
pepper
pain de campagne
butter

One hour before starting the *terrée*, soak the plank in water. Clean the mussels carefully, by scraping them with a knife and, having discarded any that are open, rinsing them two or three times in plenty of cold water.

Start with four mussels arranged in a star shape on their hinge side at the centre of the board, then cram round the others, following the same pattern, as tightly as possible so they do not open too quickly and lose their liquid. Totally bury the mussels in as many pine needles as you can.

Set the needles on fire, fanning the fire with a large piece of hardboard. The cooking time lasts for roughly 5 minutes. The mussel shells will be black with ash, and your hands will get quite dirty, for there is no other way to eat them. Eat with buttered bread and black pepper.

La mouclade de Liliane Sala

MUSSELS WITH CURRIED CREAM

2 kg/4 lb large Bouchot mussels
150 ml/¼ pint Gros-Plant wine
2 shallots, very finely chopped
2 garlic cloves, very finely chopped
1 bouquet garni
a pinch of curry powder
1 tablespoon *crème fraîche*
pepper
2 fresh basil leaves

SERVES 4

Wash and scrape the mussels, discarding any already open. Using the pointed blade of a sturdy knife, hold each one in your left hand in a cloth and open by the hinge by turning the knife. Drain off and reserve any liquid. Arrange each halved mussel in a flameproof dish which you will bring straight to the table.

Pour the mussel liquid and the wine into a pan and add the shallots, garlic and bouquet garni. Add the curry powder and bring to the boil, then reduce the heat and simmer for 5 minutes. Drain this stock through a fine sieve, add the *crème fraîche* and a grinding of pepper and pour over the mussels. Cook the mussels over medium heat for 3–4 minutes. Finely shred the basil leaves over the prepared dish and serve at once with crusty bread.

Moules marinières de Liliane Sala

FRESH MUSSEL STEW

1.5 kg/3 lb large Bouchot mussels
300 ml/½ pint dry white wine
1 tablespoon white wine vinegar
3 shallots, finely chopped
1 large garlic clove, crushed
pepper
1 bouquet garni
a knob of butter
3 basil leaves, shredded

SERVES 4

Scrape and clean the mussels. In a large pot combine all the ingredients except the mussels and basil. Bring the stock to the boil and simmer for 4 minutes. Add the mussels, cover and stirring once or twice cook quickly until all the mussels are opened. Discard any mussel which has not opened. Add the shredded basil, check the seasoning and serve at once.

Opposite: Hand-carved Saintonge kitchen furniture.

Right: La terrée – a feast on July 14th.

— CHAPTER 5 —

Central France

LIMOUSIN · AUVERGNE

Hidden away in the centre of France is the Limousin, a region famous for its Limoges porcelain, its splendid livestock and its landscape.

The three departments of the Creuse, Corrèze and Haute-Vienne form a cluster of gently rounded hills and tiny valleys where streams caper over mossy stones towards lakes filled with lilies. Here and there a remote farm, hamlet or small village nestles at the end of powdery country lanes bordered by thick hedgerows of berries and medlar trees or woods gorged with a wealth of natural foods – wild mushrooms, hazelnuts and plump chestnuts.

This is one of the less populated regions of France. If many young people have left, attracted by the urban glitter of other areas, those who have stayed seem to make the most of their habitat.

Berries are picked and made into *tourtes*, jams and *pâtes de fruit*, while summer cherries, autumn apples and purple plums are the basis for the scrumptious batter pudding *clafoutis* or thick pancakes called *flognardes*. A variety of mushrooms enter into the preparations of *omelettes campagnardes* or fricassees made with the prime-quality veal or beef of the region. Freshly caught trout is usually simply quickly fried in butter to retain its flavour and firmness. As for vegetables, cabbage, potatoes and chestnuts are mainly served boiled, braised or puréed either together or separately or combined with pork products, sometimes in the most exceptional recipes such as the chestnut black pudding I was offered by my miller friend, Renée.

Waterlilies on a Limousin lake.

To the east of the Limousin lies the vast region of the Massif Central. In gastronomic terms it is known as the Auvergne. This volcanic territory of France is vast and attractive. The air is pure, the grass is green. A land of thick forests, lakes and streams, it gives birth to the longest river in France, the Loire.

Although simple, its cuisine is known throughout France: robust, and perhaps a little crude, but it needs to be. The winters here are harsh, the villages sparse and much of the land has to be reached on foot. Auvergne is noted for its *charcuterie*. Smoked hams, dry sausage and *saucissons* adorn the market places along with the bottled offal specialities such as *tripoux*.

The region also produces four famous cheeses: they are the blue-veined Bleu d'Auvergne, the Fourme d'Ambert, Cantal and St-Nectaire, a mountain cheese with a bite of hazelnut. Cantal enters the preparation of many dishes, from soups to the famous *truffade*, made not with truffles but with potatoes, 'the truffle of the poor'.

But above all Auvergne is Le Puy and its lentils. Cultivated at an altitude of 1,000 metres, the green lentil of Le Puy is unlike any other variety. Traditionally cooked with sausages, it is the source of many local dishes. I went to Le Puy for the lentil harvest and came back full of enthusiasm about the range of cuisine involving this most esoteric and delicate of all dried vegetables.

—— Renée, the Miller's Wife ——

What else should have I expected? When I entered Renée's kitchen, the miller's wife was elbow-deep in flour making pastry. 'Finissez d'entrer,' she said in her soft rolling Limousin accent. I was amused by that regional form of welcome – 'Finish entering' – quite new to me.

The smells coming from the large stove made me feel hungry at once. They were fruity, vegetably, meaty – the reassuring combination that suggests good food is being prepared. Renée's strong hands were folding, plying, rolling with the dexterity associated only with the professional or the well-trained. Her pale blue painted kitchen had the organized appearance of a room which has been for years the domain of the perfect *maîtresse de maison*.

I was offered a refreshing glass of home-made *citronnade*, a lemon concoction in which fig, pineapple and raisins had been left to infuse, and while in the adjacent milling room the staff of life was grinding away, Renée, without stopping work for a moment, divulged the culinary secrets of the Limousin kitchen, and the art of self-sufficiency.

By the mill pond is a complete farmyard where all kinds of fowl are reared, and as in the old days, the pig is slaughtered at the beginning of each winter to provide the family with salt and smoked meat, pâtés, sausages and black puddings for the rest of the year. The black pudding of the region has very little fat content but is kept sweet and mealy by the addition of a large amount of puréed chestnuts. At no stage did Renée refer to a cookery or note book while giving me the recipes in detail. She had fed her family for forty years with the dishes of the region and was in full control of the necessary skills and techniques.

That night we were served a handsome *pâté de pommes de terre*, a potato pie so good I simply had to have a second helping. It had been preceeded by *la supa*, a beef consommé into which each of us poured a glass of red wine following the Limousin custom of *faire chabro*. We finished with home-made chestnut purée laced with Armagnac and served chilled with home-made vanilla ice-cream.

During the rest of my stay I had the chance to sample a light tomato and mustard tart, a chestnut black pudding served with sautéed apples, a dish of *haricots à la couenne* made with semi-dry haricot beans braised with the finest of slices of belly pork, rolled and left to marinate for a day or two with garlic, salt and pepper – this is in fact the local harvest dish. Another speciality I was given was a dish of roast duck served with cabbage leaves scrupulously folded around a herby stuffing. A *clafoutis* was made with the first windfall apples from the orchard, and cherries which had been bottled earlier in the year were added with Cointreau to a smooth batter for *les crêpes aux fruits*. I also learnt how to steam chestnuts *à la limousine*, keeping them moist, ready to be eaten with bread and butter dropped in a bowl of hot buttered milk or as a simple soup.

Above: Home-made chestnut black pudding.

Opposite: Near Renée's kitchen – the milling room.

Pâté de pommes de terre limousin

— POTATO PIE WITH YEAST CRUST —

YEAST DOUGH
8 g/¼ oz fresh yeast
75 ml/3 fl oz lukewarm water
500 g/1 lb plain flour
a pinch of salt
1 egg
75 g/3 oz butter, softened
75 ml/3 fl oz iced water

FILLING
500 g/1 lb minced pork
a small handful of sorrel, chopped
10–15 fresh parsley sprigs, chopped
2 garlic cloves, crushed
2 shallots, finely chopped
salt and pepper
1 kg/2 lb potatoes

— SERVES 6 —

Mash and dissolve the yeast in the lukewarm water, incorporate 100g/4oz of the flour. Mix well, shape into a ball and leave to prove, covered with a damp cloth, for 1 hour.

Sift the remaining flour and salt into a large mixing bowl and make a well in the centre. Break in the egg and add the butter and cold water. Gradually draw the flour into the central ingredients and pound in the risen yeast mixture.

Transfer the dough to a floured board and knead for about 10 minutes with the palms of your hands until the dough is smooth and elastic. Shape it into a ball and leave to prove in a warm place for 2 hours.

Preheat the oven to 220°C/425°F/gas mark 7. To make the filling, mix the pork and all the other ingredients except the potatoes together with a fork. Peel and thinly slice the potatoes.

Roll out three-quarters of the dough and line a 25 cm/9 inch deep pie dish with it, leaving a lip of pastry overlapping the rim of the dish. Layer a third of the sliced potatoes in the dish, then add a layer of the pork mixture. Repeat the layers until all the filling ingredients have been used, finishing with a little pork mixture to keep the top layer of potatoes moist. Roll out the remaining dough and

cut it into a circular lid. Cover the pie with the lid and fold the overlapping pastry on to it, pinching the edges well with dampened fingers, to seal. Make a funnel in the centre of the lid.

Place the pie in the centre of the preheated oven and bake for 20 minutes, then lower the oven temperature to 200°C/400°F/gas mark 6 and bake for a further 1 hour 10 minutes. If during cooking time the pastry browns too much cover the pie loosely with foil. Serve straight from the dish. Eat on its own with a garlicky green salad.

Tarte à la moutarde

— MUSTARD AND TOMATO TART —

1 quantity Yeast Dough
(see previous recipe)
3 tablespoons thick *crème fraîche*
2 tablespoons mild Dijon mustard
8 tomatoes, peeled
8 thin slices Cantal cheese or Gruyère
salt and pepper
a sprinkling of fresh chopped thyme

— SERVES 6 —

Preheat the oven to 220°C/425°F/gas mark 7.

Roll out the dough and use to line a large tart dish. Spread the pastry with the *crème fraîche* mixed with the mustard. Thickly slice the tomatoes on top and add the cheese, salt and pepper and thyme.

Bake in the centre of the preheated oven for 25 minutes or until the pastry is well-cooked. Serve at once, or lukewarm.

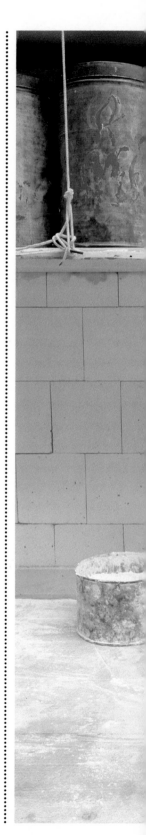

Haricots à la couenne

— BAKED HARICOT BEANS WITH PORK ROLLS —

2 kg/4 lb fresh semi-dry beans in the pod
or 1 kg/2 lb dried haricot beans
500 g/1 lb belly of pork with the rind
3 garlic cloves, finely crushed
2 heaped tablespoons chopped fresh parsley
salt and coarsely ground black pepper
1 onion studded with a clove
1 bouquet garni
1 tablespoon fresh lard

— SERVES 6 —

Pod the semi-dry beans if using. If using dried beans, soak them in cold water for 3 hours or more. Drain and rinse well before cooking.

The pork needs to be rolled into little parcels, so ask your butcher to slice it as thinly as possible. Mix the garlic with the parsley, add salt and pepper and spoon this mixture on to the pork slices. Roll up neatly, tie with butcher's string and keep refrigerated for one day.

The following day, place the pork rolls in a pot with the onion, bouquet garni and black pepper, and cover with water. Bring to the boil, then simmer, covered, for 1 hour.

Lift the pork rolls from the pot and leave the stock to cool down. When cooled, cook the beans in it for 1–1½ hours, depending on type, or until tender but not mushy.

Preheat the oven to 220°C/425°F/gas mark 7.

Melt the lard in a flameproof casserole, add the drained beans with a little of the stock, bury the pork rolls among them and check the seasoning. Cook in the preheated oven for 30 minutes or until tender.

To serve, discard the string from the pork rolls, arrange them over the beans and serve very hot with plenty of crusty bread and a full-bodied red wine.

'When I entered her kitchen, the miller's wife was elbow-deep in flour making pastry'.

Feuilles de chou farcies

—— STUFFED CABBAGE LEAVES ——

This is a labour of love and takes a long time to prepare, for each leaf has to be individually rolled.

◇

1 firm round cabbage
4 slices bread, crusts removed
a little milk
750 g/1½ lb minced pork
2 eggs, beaten
2 shallots, finely chopped
1 garlic clove, crushed
a small handful of fresh sorrel, chopped
salt and pepper
1 tablespoon lard
1 tablespoon sunflower oil
2 onions, sliced
4 young carrots, sliced

—— SERVES 6 ——

Blanch the cabbage for 8 minutes in boiling water. Leave to drain upside down in a colander and separate into individual leaves that you will pat dry with a cloth. Discard any hard stems.

Prepare the stuffing by first soaking the bread in the milk. Drain well by pressing with the hands until most of the moisture has gone. Mix well with the pork, beaten eggs, shallots, garlic, sorrel and seasoning.

Place the cabbage leaves on a flat surface. Spoon some of the stuffing inside each leaf. Fold the sides inwards and roll up the leaf from the stem end to form a neat parcel.

Heat the lard and oil in a flameproof casserole, sauté each cabbage leaf parcel on both sides until golden, add the onions and carrots and cover with water. Simmer for 1 hour, covered, reducing the stock towards the end by removing the lid. Either eat as a main dish or as an accompaniment for roast duck, goose or even pork.

'In one of the less populated regions of France, those who chose to stay seem to make the most of their habitat'.

Marrons à la Limousin

—— CHESTNUTS LIMOUSIN-STYLE ——

3 large potatoes, peeled
2 large carrots, peeled
1 stem celery or 6 slices of celeriac
500 g/1 lb peeled sweet chestnuts
the outer leaves of a fresh cabbage
water to cover

—— SERVES 6 ——

Line the base of a cast iron pot with the sliced potatoes, carrots and celery or celeriac. Pour in enough water to cover these vegetables. Place the peeled chestnuts over the bed of vegetables and cover with cabbage leaves. Simmer with the lid on in a low oven (180°C/350°F/gas mark 4) for 2 hours or until the chestnuts are tender.

To serve, discard the cabbage leaves. Lift the chestnuts from the pot and serve on their own, buttered, as a vegetable or mix with the potatoes, carrots, celery or celeriac, add a large knob of butter and serve with bread or as an accompaniment to a meat dish.

Crêpes aux cerises

—— THICK CHERRY PANCAKES ——

350 g/12 oz plain flour
a pinch of salt
4 eggs
a little milk (optional)
1 tablespoon caster sugar
500 g/1 lb bottled cherries, stoned, in syrup
2 tablespoons Grand Marnier

—— SERVES 4–6 ——

Sift the flour and salt into a mixing bowl. Make a well in the centre. Beat the eggs and pour them into the well, then slowly draw the flour into the eggs, adding a little milk if the mixture is too thick to work. Add the stoned cherries and their syrup, and the Grand Marnier. Mix well, adding a little more milk if the batter is not thin enough. Leave to rest in a cool place for 3 hours. Cook them as ordinary pancakes, making them quite thick. Serve immediately.

—— The Road to the Lentil Farm ——

I visited Le Puy on my way back from the Languedoc. The journey through the Ardèche valley was enchanting, particularly the last foray along the source of the river on a country lane between the town of Mayres and the tiny hamlet of Astet. On either side towered the mountains and around us were grapes, apples and chestnut trees.

I met a shepherd who spoke of bygone days when chestnut growing was his main occupation. The classic evening meal of times past was *le cousinat*, a soup made with dried chestnuts, milk and prunes.

I carried on towards Le Puy and the village of Brives-Charensac where I stayed with Yvonne Bernard and her husband in their old coach house. That night we ate a *gigot* of lamb marinated in red wine, and with it, of course, a dish of Le Puy lentils and sautéed mushrooms. We finished the meal with a *pachade*, a thick crêpe eaten with sweet buttered apples.

Canard aux lentilles

—— DUCK WITH LENTILS ——

1 farm or wild duck
100 g/4 oz raw smoked ham
2 garlic cloves
1 large smoked sausage (*saucisse d'Auvergne*)
1 carrot
1 onion
2 tablespoons sunflower oil
2 bouquets garnis
water
400 g/14 oz lentils
1 red cabbage
salt and pepper

—— SERVES 4 ——

Clean and truss the duck. Cut off the gland on top of the parson's nose, to avoid too strong a taste.

Finely chop the ham, garlic, sausage, carrot and onion. Heat the oil in a flameproof casserole and brown the duck on all sides. Remove from the casserole. Add the chopped ingredients and sauté until the onions are transparent. Return the duck to the pot, add a bouquet garni and a glass of water, cover and reduce the heat. Simmer for 2 hours.

Meanwhile, cook the lentils in water with a bouquet garni. Quarter the cabbage and boil separately in salted water. Drain both vegetables well.

Skim the excess rendered duck fat from the casserole and add the lentils and red cabbage.

Season with black pepper. Cover and simmer for a further 30 minutes. Carve the duck and place on a heated serving dish. Serve surrounded by the vegetable and lentil mixture.

Gigot d'agneau façon chevreuil

—— MARINATED LEG OF LAMB ——

2 kg/4 lb leg of lamb
2 onions, 1 studded with a clove
2 large carrots
1 bouquet garni
1 bottle red wine
1 garlic clove
salt and pepper
a little butter

—— SERVES 6 ——

Place the lamb in a large earthenware casserole. Place the vegetables and bouquet garni around it. Pour in the wine. Leave to marinate in a cold room for 48 hours, turning the lamb from time to time. Remove from the marinade 1 hour before roasting.

Preheat the oven to 220°C/425°F/gas mark 7. Dry the *gigot* with kitchen paper. Push a clove of garlic into the knuckle end. Lay the lamb in a large earthenware roasting dish. Season with salt and pepper and dot with butter.

Place in the oven until the surface of the lamb is brown then reduce the oven heat to 200°C/400°F/gas mark 6. Resume roasting at 15 minutes per 500 g/1 lb.

Lentilles du Puy

LE PUY LENTILS

Save the lentil-flavoured liquid from this recipe to make *Soupe du Puy (see below)*.

◇

500 g/1 lb lentils
1 glass red wine
1 onion, studded with a clove
2 fresh thyme sprigs
1 litre/1¾ pints water
salt

SERVES 6

Place the lentils and all the other ingredients except the salt in a saucepan. Bring quickly to the boil, then reduce the heat and simmer for 30–35 minutes until the lentils are tender. Season with salt towards the end of the cooking time.

Les lentilles en salade (lentil salad)
Cook the lentils as for *Lentilles du Puy*. Lift from the stock and drain well. Serve with a vinaigrette dressing and a garnish of onions and tomatoes. This salad is excellent with any cold pork produce.

Soupe du Puy

LENTIL SOUP

◇

Use the lentils' cooking stock from the previous recipe to make a soup. Add carrots, cabbage, courgette, leek, a few potatoes and a piece of streaky bacon. Cook until the vegetables are tender. Push through a sieve or blend in an electric blender, having removed the piece of bacon.

Les lentilles du vendredi

LENTILS IN A WHITE SAUCE
WITH HARD-BOILED EGGS

The people of Le Puy are staunch Catholics and do not eat meat on a Friday. This dish of lentils is the traditional Friday lunch.

◇

Cook the lentils as for *Lentilles du Puy*. Serve them tossed in a *sauce béchamel* and garnished with chopped hard-boiled eggs and parsley.

Right: A home-cured ham in a Le Puy lacemaker's home.

La pachade

PANCAKE WITH SAUTÉED APPLES

100 g/4 oz plain flour
a pinch of salt
2 eggs
275 ml/9 fl oz milk
2 teaspoons Cognac
butter for frying

ACCOMPANIMENT
75 g/3 oz unsalted butter
1 kg/2 lb dessert apples, peeled, cored and sliced
100 g/4 oz caster sugar

SERVES 4–6

Sift the flour with the salt into a mixing bowl. Make a well in the centre and break in the eggs. Add a touch of milk and start drawing the flour into the eggs, gradually adding the remaining milk. Work well to avoid lumps. Add the Cognac and leave the batter to rest for 1 hour or more.

Twenty minutes before cooking the pancake, cook the apples. Melt the butter in a frying pan. As soon as it starts to foam, add the apples, mixing well to coat them with butter. Lower the heat and cook for 20 minutes or until the apples are tender. Sprinkle with the sugar while still in the pan.

Cook the *pachade*. Melt some butter in a large frying pan. Pour the batter in all at once and cook on one side, reducing the heat, then turn and cook on the other side. Spread the apples over the pancake and serve in slices.

— CHAPTER 6 —

The South-West

GUYENNE · GASCONY

The two ancient provinces of Guyenne and Gascony are a legendary bastion of French gastronomy. They embrace the Bordelais with its noble wines, the Sarladais, a truffle paradise, the Périgord and the Landes, domains of *foie gras* and *confit d'oie*, the Rouergue, land of Roquefort cheese and Armagnac.

These are only the primary landmarks on the gastronomic map of the region. One really needs to comb through each area to discover and appreciate just how many places are connected with food of special note. The search can be infinite.

First there is Bordeaux, the port and capital of Guyenne with its noble architecture still graced by some Louis XVI buildings. The food there gives total priority to the use of wine. Eggs, fish, the simplest cut of meat or the excellent poultry of the region are all adorned with the rich *sauce Bordelaise*, based on a roux made with chopped shallots, moistened with a good Bordeaux wine and simmered with herbs and the addition of a little marrow from a veal bone.

In the neighbouring wine communities the cockerel is no longer served simply *au vin* but becomes a more sophisticated *coq au St-Estèphe* or *coq au St-Emilion*. In Périgueux, another antique city where the Roman mingles with the Byzantine, not only are there *foie gras* and truffles but also a local *potée* called *sobronade* and a dish of veal studded with ham, gherkins and anchovies and delicately braised in white wine.

It is among the feudal villages of the Dordogne such as Bergerac and Sarlat that the potato becomes *sarladaise*, baked in the oven with a touch of garlic, or *confite*, sautéed in just enough goose fat to brown each slice and served with a garlicky *persillade*.

Travel into the Quercy, drink Vin de Cahors, an unusually earthy wine, by the towers of the ancient Pont Valentre, sample the local soups, *tourins*, made with tomatoes and chicken, or *à l'aoucou* with goose neck. You will also find *estouffades*, pork with beans, tripe with saffron and a rich *lièvre farci en Cabessal* – a hare stuffed with veal, pork and ham and braised inside a round earthenware dish in herbs and red wine.

From there discover the Agenais, the land of prunes and the fruit's endless culinary usage. Sit under the vaulted squares of twelfth-century stately built villages – *les bastides* – such as Castillonnes, and savour the unusual simplicity of eggs fried in goose fat, and *cèpes*, the king of fungi, cooked in a broth, grilled with shallots and garlic or set into a moist omelette.

Amble along the river Baïse into the town of Nérac, seat of Henri de Navarre, and ask for a terrine of partridges cooked for hours with ham, truffles and herbs. Venture to the Huguenot city of Montauban where all around prime vegetables grow on terraced fields and find your way through the Aveyron valley known as *la vieille France*

Preparing vegetables in the shade of the garden in Gascony.

gourmande. There you will savour rich game pâtés, *salmis* of wild pigeon, *poules noires* stuffed with chestnuts, trout grilled with herbs and rabbit cooked with capers and tiny onions.

A step further, in the Rouergue, you will reach Rodez, a proud city of Gothic grandeur and nearby, Roquefort and the finest of blue veined cheese made with ewe's milk, as well as lamb braised with fragrant juniper berries found on the surrounding hills.

The journeying is not over for it would be a pity to miss the Gers, land of d'Artagnan, and Auch, the capital of Gascony, set in an immense landscape of hillocks and knolls with distant views towards the Pyrénées mountains. There you will be given a *cassoulet* made with fresh broad beans, regarded by the older generation as the original *cassoulet*, and also a spicy *compote de poule*,

boiling fowl simmered with herbs and spices until it falls off the bone.

Finally, make your way towards the Atlantic coast through Mont-de-Marsan and the immense pine forest of the Landes and enjoy the *salade landaise* made with *confit de canard* and *foie gras*, or a simple *daube de canard*, a braised farm duck. Also eel cooked in red wine with prunes and along the coast towards the dunes of Arcachon, the traditional way of eating oysters with freshly grilled sausages and a glass of iced sweet Sauternes – a little esoteric maybe, but an interesting experience for the tastebuds.

I entered the region by the barren Causses and the revered town of Rocamadour. After an *al fresco* lunch of *tomme de chèvre* and fresh walnuts in a wild walnut orchard, I spent the next few days in the kitchens of dedicated cooks.

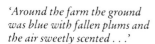

'Around the farm the ground was blue with fallen plums and the air sweetly scented . . .'

—— The Plums of Agen ——

It was not far from Agen, in the small village of Douzains, that I visited a farm where plums are grown organically and prunes prepared traditionally. The entire Bousquet family are devoted fruit growers, and the morning I called their son-in-law had just devised a new recipe of semi-dried plums stoned and filled with a hand-pounded paste of fresh hazelnuts, sugar and a little *eau-de-vie*. This delicacy would join others for sale at the farm shop, such as prunes in spiced white wine, or macerated in Armagnac, and a dry and delectable *eau-de-vie de prune* distilled on the premises. All

around the farm the ground was blue with fallen fruit and the air sweetly scented with the perfume of cooking plums.

I had been invited for lunch and in the kitchen Madame Bousquet was attending to a prune stuffing for the roast chicken. She was also waiting to demonstrate the preparation of a very traditional regional dessert – in her case, according to her grandmother's recipe – *la tourtière*, a fine pastry case filled with apples, prunes and *eau-de-vie*. A little tricky to prepare, but quite unlike any other fruit tart.

Tourtière de Mémée

— GRANNY'S APPLE AND PRUNE PIE —

Prepare the dough the previous night.

◇

DOUGH
500 g/1 lb plain flour
a pinch of salt
1 egg
4 tablespoons sunflower oil
iced water (optional)
2 tablespoons lard

FILLING
10 cubes of brown sugar
40 g/1½ oz caster sugar
3 tablespoons *eau-de-vie-de-prune*
1 cooking apple, peeled and sliced
12 large prunes, stoned and soaked

— SERVES 4–6 —

Make the pastry dough: sift the flour and salt on to a large wooden board and make a well in the centre. Beat the egg with the oil and pour into the well. Using the fingertips, draw the flour quickly into the mixture, until a soft dough is formed, adding a little water if necessary. Knead the dough for about 5 minutes until smooth, shape into a ball, cover with a damp cloth and leave to rest in a cool place overnight.

The following day, flour a work surface and using the heel of both hands and starting at the centre, flatten the dough, then pull at it with your fingertips until a huge thin square is obtained.

Melt the lard. Dip a goose feather or pastry brush into the melted lard and sprinkle some lard all over the dough. Fold in three. Sprinkle with more lard, fold in three again and repeat once more. Wrap the dough in greaseproof paper and leave for 20 minutes.

Preheat the oven to 200°C/400°F/gas mark 6.

Quickly roll out three-quarters of the dough and use to line a 25 cm/10 inch pie dish. Arrange the sugar lumps and caster sugar on the dough and sprinkle with some *eau-de-vie*. Add the sliced apple, sprinkle with more *eau-de-vie*, then add the prunes. Roll out the remaining pastry, cover the fruit and seal the edges carefully. Bake the *tourtiere* in the preheated oven for 30–40 minutes until the pastry is golden-brown and light. Serve lukewarm.

Farce aux pruneaux pour poulet

— PRUNE STUFFING FOR ROAST FOWL —

300 g/10 oz prunes, stoned
150 g/5 oz bread, crust removed
125 ml/4 fl oz milk
the chicken liver
1 tablespoon Armagnac
1 egg
a pinch of dried thyme
salt and pepper

Soak the prunes in water overnight. Soak the bread in the milk. Squeeze out excess moisture and place in a bowl with the other ingredients. Chop the prunes coarsely and fold them in. Cover and leave to rest in the refrigerator for 2 hours. Spoon inside the chicken and truss it before roasting as usual.

Farce pour oie à l'agenaise

— STUFFING FOR ROAST GOOSE —

20 prunes, stoned
225 g/8 oz fresh belly of pork, rind removed
1 bouquet garni
1 onion
2 shallots
25 g/1 oz butter
200 g/7 oz bread, crusts removed
125 ml/4 fl oz milk
12 green olives, stoned and chopped
pepper
2 egg yolks

Soak the prunes overnight. Cook the belly pork in salted water with the bouquet garni for 45 minutes. Drain, leave to cool and mince coarsely. Finely chop the onion and shallots and sauté them in the butter until transparent. Leave to cool, then add to the minced pork. Soak the bread in the milk, then squeeze out the excess. Add the chopped olives and black pepper to the minced pork mixture with the egg yolks and bread. Mash well with a fork. Finally add the drained whole prunes. Mix well with the hands and spoon into the goose cavity. Truss the bird, cover with kitchen foil and leave for one day in the refrigerator before cooking.

—— A Handful of Truffles ——

From Agen I travelled up towards Périgueux for an intriguing outing in a small wooded hamlet. A note had been pushed through my door in the late evening. 'If you want to come truffle digging, be at the farm at the bottom of the hill at dawn'.

I woke with excitement. It was like having a secret rendezvous with a gold digger! After all, truffles are almost as expensive as gold. One reads of black and brown nuggets, of dealers dressed in sombre suits in market places, of precious little bags being passed under the table in clandestine French cafés. Was I going to be sworn to secrecy?

A serene-looking young woman was at the farm gate. By her stood a small white dog. Only the sight of the hatchet at her waist and the cotton bag in her right hand made me realize that I was looking at a truffle hunter.

We walked through the hills. The dog worked hard at scratching the promised ground. Truffles were found.

On our return I was not sworn to secrecy but instead met in a warm welcoming kitchen by Jeanne's mother who swiftly placed a large truffle omelette on the table. 'A reward for getting up so early,' she said. In silence we ate the fluffy eggs set around fine slivers of the heavily perfumed fungus. With it we drank fresh water from the spring. No flavour was impaired. Pure ambrosia.

I stayed with the same family for several days. Mamette, the mother, Jeanne her married daughter, ceramicist husband and children all live in the same house, a magnificent rambling stone building. It has a wing on either side of the main structure and an ornate wrought-iron balcony on to which one can step from every room including the bedrooms. Outside, a long drive through the wild garden leads to the main road bordered by walnut trees, tobacco fields, asparagus fields and vineyards.

The atmosphere is very relaxed; lots of family and friends come and go at all times. Not once were we the same number around the table at mealtimes. One sensed that behind the artistic, slightly bohemian atmosphere, somebody kept firm control. It did not take long to realize that it was Mamette, who with Jeanne had put together the small truffle canning business.

I learnt a great deal about the Périgord from this small, stocky lady, and when we visited the cellar it occurred to me that to help make entertaining seemingly easy the two women work very hard all year round, bottling and preserving every available food product from their surroundings.

Glazed crocks were lined up on a shelf, each one holding a different *confit*, or pressed meat. Goose, duck, pork, turkey, and boiling fowl are all preserved in this way and either the meat or the deliciously flavoured fat which surrounds it proves to be a useful standby when it comes to feeding hungry, unannounced guests.

I left Jeanne and her family with a few tips for my future entertaining . . .

The truffle hunter.

Omelette aux truffes

TRUFFLE OMELETTE

Truffles are preserved in a little brandy.
Add the preserving juice to the eggs for extra flavour.

◇

1 truffle
40 g/1½ oz goose fat or butter
12 eggs
truffle juice

SERVES 6

Slice the truffle thinly and sauté the slices for a few minutes in the melted goose fat or butter in a large non-stick frying pan. Beat the eggs and add the truffle juice. Pour over the truffle and cook until just set. Serve at once.

Confit

COUNTRY MEAT PRESERVE

◇

The principle is the same, whichever meat is used. In the case of a goose, duck or other fowl nothing is wasted. The giblets and wings which do not feature in the preparation of the *confit* are used for a regional fricassée, called *alicot* or *alicuit*. A thick soup is made with the uncooked carcass.

Confit d'oie

SALTED PRESERVED GOOSE

1 goose
100 g/4 oz coarse sea salt
1 tablespoon black pepper
6 bayleaves
1 tablespoon dried thyme
2 kg/4 lb lard or goose fat

SERVES 6

Trim the meat from the backbone of the goose. Remove the neck, wings and offal. Cut the meat into large pieces and rub each piece with salt. Put in an earthenware pot with the pepper, bayleaves and thyme and leave in a cool place for 36 hours.

Wipe the excess salt from each piece. Place some melted lard or goose fat at the base of a large cast iron pot, add the pieces of goose and start cooking over very low heat. The meat will eventually brown. Add more fat, cover and resume the cooking as slowly as possible for 2 hours or until the goose is very tender.

Place some more rendered fat at the base of a preserving jar. Pack the pieces of goose on top, pouring some fat over each one as you go. Tap the jar up and down so that there is no air left. Pour in more fat to cover completely. Oil a piece of greaseproof paper and tie it around the jar. The *confit* will keep for months in a cool place.

The *confit* can either be eaten cold with *pommes de terre confites* and a salad of spinach or *frisée* lettuce or it can be used for the preparation of a *cassoulet* or in a *tourte* – a pie made with salsify or tomatoes. It is also excellent reheated with a fresh chestnut purée.

Soupe de carcasse d'oie

SOUP MADE WITH GOOSE CARCASS

The same soup can be made with duck, turkey, etc.

◇

1 goose carcass
1 onion, chopped
2 garlic cloves
1 bouquet garni
1.5 litres/2½ pints water
½ celeriac, cubed
5 carrots, diced
5 potatoes, diced
1 small cabbage

SERVES 6

Put the goose carcass into a large saucepan. Add the onion, garlic and bouquet garni. Cover with the water and bring to the boil, skimming the surface as the scum rises. Add the other vegetables except the cabbage. Bring quickly to the boil, then lower the heat and simmer gently for 1½ hours.

Divide the cabbage into 6 pieces. Add to the broth and cook for a further 30 minutes. Remove the carcass. Serve the soup very hot with slices of toasted bread rubbed with oil and garlic.

Alicot

GOOSE FRICASSEE

A small fricassee for 2 people, to make use of the goose trimmings. It is in fact so good that I recommend buying poultry trimmings to make it in a larger quantity.

◇

2 teaspoons goose fat
100 g/4 oz smoked ham or smoked bacon, cubed
500 g/1 lb goose or other poultry trimmings
6 small carrots
3 onions, chopped
4 garlic cloves, chopped
2 teaspoons plain flour
1 large glass of white wine
a ladleful of broth (from the soup)
1 bouquet garni
2 teaspoons tomato purée
salt and pepper
225 g/8 oz small new potatoes, peeled

SERVES 4–6

Preheat the oven to 180°C/350°F/gas mark 4.

Heat the goose fat in a flameproof casserole. Sauté the ham and poultry until brown on all sides. Set aside and quickly seal the carrots, onions and garlic. Return the meat to the pot, sprinkle with the flour and mix well. Let the flour take colour, then cover with wine and broth. Add the bouquet garni, tomato purée and salt and pepper.

Cover and cook in the preheated oven for 2 hours, adding a little more broth if the sauce reduces too quickly. Boil the new potatoes and add to the casserole 10 minutes before serving. Uncover the dish, increase the oven heat to 220°C/425°F/gas mark 7, and let the sauce bubble for a few minutes. Serve with chopped parsley and a good *vin de pays*.

Pommes de terre confites

SAUTÉED POTATOES WITH GARLIC

1 kg/2 lb good waxy potatoes
75 g/3 oz goose fat
2 garlic cloves, crushed
2 tablespoons finely chopped parsley
sea salt
black pepper

SERVES 6

Peel and wash the potatoes. Dry them well and slice into regular slices. Heat the goose fat over high heat in a large frying pan. When it foams add the potatoes. Mix well so that each potato gets coated with fat. Add the crushed garlic and parsley, mix well and cover the pan. Lower the heat and cook gently, turning the potatoes every 5 minutes until golden brown on all sides. Replace the lid each time. Cook until tender. Season with freshly ground sea salt and black pepper.

Family home in Périgord.

Irresistible gourmandizing continued through the kitchens of Cahors, where I was given a lunch of monkfish simmered in red Vin de Cahors with truffles. In the Rouergue I dined off Roquefort tart, and veal and calf liver parcels baked with juniper berries. And to finish, grapes served with huge cloves of fresh . . . garlic! Finally, near St-Martin d'Armagnac, I visited a friend I had not seen in seven years. After a self-imposed day of fasting and lots of swimming in their pool we totally exhausted the possibilities of eating and drinking in Gascony.

—— Cherry Tomatoes for Breakfast ——

I had not seen Anne since her announcement that she had a new husband, a new house and a complete new way of life. One thing I would never have associated with her were her new hobbies: gardening and cooking. In Paris she belonged to the *petit café noir*-and-nothing-else brigade and had a maid who did everything for her including preparing meals. She swore she would never leave the capital, certainly not to go and bury herself in the country.

But there I found her, amongst the bliss of near self-sufficiency, digging her home-grown new potatoes, feeding the rabbits and taking me into a large kitchen which looked as though it had been equipped by five generations of devoted cooks. There was an Aga cooker, a scullery with every imaginable pot and pan, a permanently fixed mouli for home-made tomato *coulis* and a large second-hand wood restaurant refrigerator in which I found home-made terrines, *confits* and *rillettes*.

Country life had been a revelation for Anne, and I followed her enthusiasm for *la vie à la campagne* to the point where I found myself with her, at the crack of dawn in the vegetable garden, eating just-picked cherry tomatoes for breakfast while watching the sun rise over the distant hills.

Among the delicious things she prepared, I remember with relish a *gasconnade de jarrets d'agneau*, tender lamb knuckles braised in wine with anchovies. Also, a *garbure* – chicken soup served with slices of cold omelette and small chicken liver dumplings. One night, Anne surpassed herself with a *perdrix à la paysanne*, a partridge braised with cabbage, ham from the Landes and country sausage. It was followed by prunes in Armagnac served as a dessert with strong vanilla-flavoured home-made ice-cream. It would have been such a pity if she had never found her true talent. Here are her recipes with others gathered throughout Gascony . . .

Above: Making tomato coulis in the scullery.

Lotte au vin de Cahors

MONKFISH IN CAHORS WINE

3 carrots
3 onions
2 celery sticks
100 g/4 oz butter
salt and pepper
1.25 kg/2½ lb monkfish tails, trimmed and cleaned
1 truffle
4 slices unsmoked streaky bacon
½ bottle Vin de Cahors
water

SERVES 6

Wash, peel and cut the carrots, onions and celery into julienne strips. Heat 50 g/2 oz of the butter in a deep pan and sweat the julienne of vegetables until almost tender. Season with salt and pepper and put to one side.

Preheat the oven to 200°C/400°F/gas mark 6.

Stud the fish with pieces of truffle and wrap the bacon around the monkfish tails. Secure with butcher's string. Grease a deep flameproof baking dish with butter. Cover the base with the vegetables. Place the fish over the vegetables and pour in enough wine and water to fill two-thirds of the dish. Bring quickly to the boil over high heat. Cover with foil and cook in the preheated oven for 45 minutes.

To serve, carefully lift the fish out of the dish and place over a rack to drain. Remove and discard the bacon. To finish the sauce, pour the cooking liquid through a fine strainer into a pan and bring to the boil until it reduces. Whisk in the remaining butter, little by little, until a smooth sauce is obtained. Check the seasoning. Transfer the fish to a heated serving platter and pour the sauce over it.

Paupiettes de Rouergue

VEAL AND LIVER PARCELS
WITH JUNIPER BERRIES

Slowly baked in their own juices,
these are very succulent served with puréed potatoes.

◇

4 thin slices unsmoked back bacon, rind removed
salt and pepper
4 thin pork escalopes
4 very thin slices pig's liver
16 juniper berries
1 heaped tablespoon goose fat

SERVES 4

Lay the bacon slices on a wooden board. Season with pepper. Place a pork escalope over each bacon slice. Season the pork with a little salt. Now place the liver over the pork. Add 4 juniper berries to the centre of each and roll into small parcels. Secure each with a wooden skewer. Leave in a cool place for 1 hour.

Preheat the oven to 190°C/375°F/gas mark 5.

Grease the base of an earthenware baking dish with a little goose fat. Arrange the *paupiettes* in the dish. Dot some goose fat over each one. Bake in the preheated oven for 30 minutes. Reduce the oven heat to 160°C/325°F/gas mark 3 and bake for a further 1½ hours or until the meat feels tender when a skewer is inserted into the centre. Turn the *paupiettes* from time to time. Serve with the cooking juices.

'Anne's kitchen looked as though it had been equipped by five generations of devoted cooks.'

A Bordeaux kitchen.

Tourte au Roquefort

ROQUEFORT CHEESE TART

200 g/7 oz plain flour
a pinch of salt
50 g/2 oz butter
3 tablespoons iced water
50 g/2 oz lard
1 egg yolk
225 g/8 oz Roquefort cheese
pepper

SERVES 4

Place the flour and salt in a mixing bowl. Dice half the butter and rub it in with your fingertips. Add enough water to form a dough. Shape the dough into a ball and chill for 30 minutes.

Transfer the dough to a floured work surface and roll out into an oblong. Dot half of the lard over the upper two-thirds of the dough. Fold the unused third upwards, the greased third downwards, turn the dough and roll it out into an oblong. Now dot two-thirds of the dough with the remaining butter. Fold as before and roll into an oblong. Repeat the process a third time, finishing with the remaining lard this time. Chill the dough for 15 minutes.

Preheat the oven to 220°C/425°F/gas mark 7.

Roll the dough out 2 cm/¾ inch thick. Using a 23 cm/9 inch plate as a guideline, cut the dough into a circle. Using a sharp knife, trace another circle at the centre to form a lid, making sure that you do not cut all the way through the pastry. Glaze with the egg yolk mixed with water.

Transfer to a greased baking sheet and bake in the preheated oven for 35 minutes or until golden-brown and well risen. When the pastry is cooked, detach the lid and crumble the Roquefort cheese inside the pastry base. Season with freshly ground pepper. Lower the oven heat to 180°C/350°F/gas mark 4. Replace the lid and put the tart in the oven for 10 minutes. The cheese will melt inside the pastry. Serve at once.

La garbure gasconne à l'omelette et aux farcis

GASCONY SOUP WITH OMELETTE
AND CHICKEN LIVER DUMPLINGS

An ideal winter main course.

◇

SOUP

1 tablespoon goose fat
2 onions, chopped
½ small green cabbage, quartered
2 leeks, sliced
4 small carrots, diced
1 garlic clove
1 litre/1¾ pints home-made chicken stock
225 g/8 oz *confit d'oie*, diced
salt and pepper

DUMPLINGS

3 slices of bread, crusts removed
125 ml/4 fl oz milk
2 teaspoons sunflower oil
225 g/8 oz chicken livers
2 eggs, beaten
2 garlic cloves, crushed
2 teaspoons finely chopped parsley
salt and pepper

OMELETTE

4 eggs
2 teaspoons chopped chives
salt and pepper
2 teaspoons goose fat

SERVES 4

Heat the goose fat in a flameproof casserole and sauté the onions and cabbage until transparent and limp. Add the other vegetables and the garlic, toss well and pour in the chicken stock. Add the pieces of *confit d'oie*, check the seasoning and simmer for 1 hour.

To make the dumplings, soak the bread in the milk. Squeeze out the extra moisture. Heat the oil in a frying pan and sauté the chicken livers until just golden but still pink in the middle. Transfer with the bread to a mixing bowl, add the beaten eggs, garlic, parsley and seasoning. Mash well with a fork. Roll into small balls in the palms of your hands. Chill for 15 minutes. Poach in the soup 15 minutes before serving.

To make the omelette, beat the eggs with the chives and add seasoning. Cook the omelette in the hot goose fat until set. Cut into squares and add to the soup at the very last minute.

Gasconnade de jarrets d'agneau

BRAISED LAMB'S KNUCKLES

Ask your butcher to prepare 6 small knuckle ends of leg of lamb.

◇

2 tablespoons sunflower oil
6 lamb's knuckles
4 tablespoons tomato purée
1 tablespoon plain flour
2 onions, chopped
2 shallots, chopped
4 carrots, diced
1 leek, sliced
1 turnip, diced
4 garlic cloves, crushed
12 anchovy fillets
1 bottle red wine
salt and pepper
3 large tomatoes

SERVES 6

Preheat the oven to 160°C/325°F/gas mark 3.

Heat the oil in a large cast iron or flameproof casserole and brown the meat on all sides. Remove from the pan and coat each knuckle with tomato purée. Return to the pan and sauté until the coating starts to 'caramelize'. Sprinkle with flour, add all the chopped vegetables except the tomatoes, crushed garlic cloves and the anchovies. Mix well. Add the wine and plenty of black pepper. Cover and cook in the preheated oven for 4 hours. Remove the casserole from the oven. Increase the oven to 200°C/400°F/gas mark 6.

Transfer the lamb knuckles to an earthenware baking dish. Strain the cooking juices through a fine sieve. Peel the tomatoes and coarsely chop them over the meat. Sprinkle with the remaining crushed garlic. Add the cooking juices and check the seasoning. When the oven is hot enough, bake the *gasconnade* for 30–40 minutes. Serve with a *dish of Pommes de terre confites (see page 88)*, sliced potatoes deliciously browned in a little goose fat.

Sauce bordelaise, poulet au St-Estèphe, coq au St-Emilion . . . each time a good bottle of wine goes in the pot.

— CHAPTER 7 —

The Pyrénées

Three hundred kilometres of France and two very distinctive cultures – the Basque and the Catalan – are linked by the most gracious of mountain ranges: the Pyrénées. From the foothills to the peaks, their eurhythmic structure rises from the long western plain. On either side, the sea. If the temperamental Atlantic ocean dictates the wet climate of the Basque country, the Catalan-speaking Roussillon basks in the warmth of the Mediterranean sea, through fertile valleys all the way to the top of the imposing Mont Canigou.

The Pyrénées, most gracious of mountain ranges.

Characters are different. The Basque is reserved and independent. The Catalan is overt, jovial, sometimes outrageous. In between, the *patois*-speaking Pyrenean is measured, softly spoken and welcoming.

The Basque country struck me as being red and green. Green pastureland in one of the wettest regions of France, red shutters and roofs on look-alike houses, red cummerbunds and berets of the *pelota* players, red peppers hung to dry on barn walls, red sauces dominated by the constant use of tomatoes and peppers served on the red and green tablecloths of woven Basque linen.

The food, although very good, brought no surprises. It was all *à la basquaise*, from the *piperade*, an egg and peppers mixture I had for lunch, to the *poulet basquaise*, a chicken and pepper fricassee enhanced by the addition of a chili-spiced sausage similar in taste to the Spanish *chorizo*. The country-cured ham at Bayonne was as fine as its reputation but the fresh tuna which followed was once again dominated by the hot tangy taste of the green and red peppers. I was probably unlucky – the weather was desperately bad – and the heavy rain stopped me exploring the

tiny villages hung all along the mountain tracks where I had hoped to find unusual variations on the regional cuisine.

In nearby Béarn, a verdant area dominated by the ancient city of Pau, I was given a solid vegetable soup, *la garbure* prepared with *confit* and goose fat, game cooked with Armagnac and the local version of *poule au pot* – a firm boiling fowl simmered with vegetables, served with a walnut and garlic sauce – a favourite dish in the region since the reign of Henri IV, King of France and Navarre, who insisted that every French family should enjoy a chicken on Sundays.

In the Roussillon and Pyrénées Orientales goose fat gave way to olive oil. Inland, fresh trout and lamb is spiced with wild herbs and fragrant juniper berries gathered among the rocky hills and, along the coast, dishes such as *l'oulade* or *faves à l'estofat* are reminders of Spanish Catalonian cuisine.

In search of more hidden specialities, I drove into the enclave of the Ariège and the Aude. There I found peaceful landscapes, lonely lakes, ancient villages set along mountain rivers and gastronomy and social mores which are the same as a hundred years ago.

—— The First *Cèpe* of the Year ——

I was on my way to Carcassonne when I fell under the spell of the medieval town of Mirepoix. With its green main square surrounded by half-hung buildings and carved beams it is a gem and totally unlike any other southern town. That night I ate a *poularde farcie, sauce aillade* at the local *auberge*. The bird was stuffed with delicate meats and olives and served with a sauce made of parsley, walnut oil and walnuts. At the next table, a couple were eating a *cassoulet*. We talked and I ended up staying on their farm in the hills of Puivert for a couple of days.

I explored the nearby countryside, the villages with flat-fronted churches which cling to the foothills of the Pyrénées. I followed the river Aude through national parkland into the mountains towards the skiing resort of Font-Romeu. There I made my way towards the Lac des Bouillouses and joined the Sunday mushroom pickers among rocky streams, wild horses and pine trees. I picked some *cèpes des pins*, tiny yellow fungus, and, in the woods below, a hatful of juniper berries.

On my return Jacqueline made a regional garlic soup, *tourin*, also known as *aïgo* in the local *patois*. It was due to be followed by a roast chicken which was soon turned into a *poulet aux cèpes* when I emptied the contents of my basket on to the kitchen table. We finished our meal with some *fromage de chèvre* made by Yves the previous day and a wholesome pear pie, *la croustade du Couserans*.

After dinner we studded a saddle of lamb with some of my juniper berries. The perfumed meat was spit-roasted on the open fire the following evening. As a first course that night we ate one of Jacqueline's recipes, *la mousse de chèvre frais*.

Tourin de l'Ariège

GARLIC SOUP THICKENED WITH EGG

1 litre/1¾ pints water
2 teaspoons white wine vinegar
6 large garlic cloves
2 eggs
½ teaspoon mustard
2 tablespoons sunflower oil
salt
4 slices stale *pain de campagne*

SERVES 4

Bring the water and vinegar to the boil in a saucepan. Chop the garlic coarsely and throw it into the pan. Cook for 20 minutes. Separate the eggs. Using a fork, beat the egg whites into the soup. Cook for a further 10 minutes.

Beat the egg yolks in a bowl with the mustard. Add the oil drop by drop, beating vigorously until a mayonnaise is formed. Pour a ladleful of garlic *bouillon* into the bowl, mix well and pour into the soup away from the heat. Check the seasoning. Pour into individual soup plates over a slice of stale bread.

Poulet aux cèpes

CHICKEN WITH CÈPES

500 g/1 lb *cèpes*
3 tablespoons olive oil
1 small garlic clove, crushed
1 shallot, chopped
40 g/1½ oz butter
1 chicken
salt and pepper
2 tablespoons port
1 tablespoon chopped parsley

SERVES 4

Clean the *cèpes* with kitchen paper and cut off the earthy stems. Cut the *cèpes* into thick slices. Heat some of the oil in a frying pan and sauté the *cèpes* for 6 minutes with the garlic and shallot.

Heat the remaining oil and the butter in a flameproof casserole and brown the whole chicken on all sides. Cover, reduce the heat and cook slowly for 20 minutes per 500 g/1 lb, turning the chicken from time to time so that it does not burn. After 20 minutes add the *cèpes* to the casserole, together with the sautéed shallot and garlic. Season with salt and pepper.

When the chicken is cooked, carve and transfer to a heated serving dish with the *cèpes*. Pour the port into the casserole. Scrape up the pan juices with the port. Bring the sauce to the boil and spoon over the chicken and *cèpes*. Serve at once, sprinkled with the parsley.

La mousse de chèvre frais

FRESH GOAT'S CHEESE MOUSSE

You will need one individual earthenware ramekin per person.

◇

4 slices bread
2 *chèvre frais* cheeses (total weight 500 g/1 lb)
2 teaspoons tomato purée
salt and pepper
3 tablespoons crème fraîche
herbes de Provence
4 teaspoons virgin olive oil

SERVES 4

Preheat the oven to its maximum.

Cut each slice of bread into a circle to fit the base of a ramekin. Toast the bread circles on both sides. Place one at the bottom of each ramekin.

Beat the cheese with the tomato purée and add salt and pepper. Spoon a quarter of the mixture into each ramekin. Spoon the *crème fraîche* over, sprinkle with *herbes de Provence* and pour 1 teaspoon of olive oil on top of each ramekin. Place in the hot oven until the oil starts sizzling. Serve immediately.

Selle de mouton au genièvre

SADDLE OF LAMB WITH JUNIPER BERRIES

◇

Ask your butcher to bone and roll the saddle of lamb. Twenty-four hours before cooking the meat, stud it all over with plenty of juniper berries. Rub some olive oil over it. Sprinkle with freshly ground black pepper. Partially wrap with greaseproof paper and leave in a cold place.

To cook, spit roast, allowing 20 minutes per 500 g/1 lb, basting very frequently. Serve with a green salad.

Poularde farcie, sauce aillade

BOILED FOWL WITH OIL,
WALNUT AND GARLIC SAUCE

100 g/4 oz green olives, pitted
3 slices raw mountain ham
1 garlic clove
225 g/8 oz coarsely minced pork
1 egg
salt and pepper
1 large boiling fowl
2 celery sticks
1 onion
1 bouquet garni
200 ml/7 fl oz white wine

SAUCE
2 garlic cloves
5 tablespoons walnut oil
juice of ½ lemon
2 tablespoons finely chopped parsley
10 walnut kernels, crushed
2 tablespoons chicken stock

———————— SERVES 6 ————————

Soak the olives in cold water for 30 minutes. Dry and chop coarsely. Cut the ham into very small cubes. Crush the garlic. Place the olives, ham and garlic in a large mixing bowl with the minced pork, egg and black pepper. Mix well with your hands.

Spoon the stuffing inside the bird. Truss securely with needle and thread. Place the bird in a large saucepan and add the celery, onion and bouquet garni. Cover with water, bring quickly to the boil and skim the surface once or twice. Reduce the heat, add the wine and cook gently for 2 hours or until the chicken is tender.

Just before serving, prepare the sauce. Crush the garlic and fold it into a vinaigrette sauce made with the walnut oil, lemon juice, parsley and crushed walnuts. Add the chicken stock. Whisk well and serve in a separate gravy boat with the fowl.

La croustade aux poires

PEAR PIE

225 g/8 oz plain flour
a pinch of salt
1½ teaspoons baking powder
3 eggs
150 g/5 oz caster sugar
200 g/7 oz unsalted butter, softened
500 g/1 lb firm pears
1 vanilla pod
1 tablespoon iced water

———————— SERVES 6 ————————

Sift the flour, salt and baking powder on to a large wooden board. Make a well in the centre. Break the eggs into the well. Using the fingertips, work the eggs with 2 tablespoons of the sugar. Gradually draw in the flour until a dough is formed. Transfer the dough to a floured worktop and knead until smooth and elastic. Stretch the dough with your hands into a thin oblong. Dot one-third of the butter over the dough. Fold the pastry in three. Roll out into an oblong and repeat the process twice with the remaining butter. Leave to rest at room temperature for 1 hour.

Meanwhile, poach the pears with 50 g/2 oz of the sugar and the vanilla pod. When they are tender, lift from the pan and reduce the juice to a minimum. Remove the vanilla pod.

Preheat the oven to 200°C/400°F/gas mark 6.

Roll out two-thirds of the dough and use to line a greased deep pie dish. Sprinkle the remaining sugar over the dough and pile the fruit inside the dish. Drizzle over the reduced pear juice. Roll out the remaining pastry, cover the fruit with it and seal the edges. Make a funnel at the centre with a small piece of rolled foil. Bake in the preheated oven for 30 minutes or until the crust is cooked and crisp. Eat cold or lukewarm.

The boisterous tramontane wind blows through the cherry orchards at Céret, in the Roussillon.

—— Cherries, Matisse, Chagall and Picasso ——

I left the Ariège and entered the Roussillon, the driest and sunniest part of France, through sleepy backroads. From Quillan I followed the course of the St-Bertrand river, through the mountainous Col de St-Louis, dropping suddenly on to the soft pink houses of the picturesque village of Caudies-de-Fenouillèdes. The surrounding vineyards were already tinged with their autumn colours ranging from powdery pink to the richest of crimsons. The heavy black clusters of grapes were hanging off each vine, but not for long, for the grape-picking season had already started. Soon the Fitou and earthy Roussillon wines would be ready.

Voyaging through more tortuous mountain roads, and even more picturesque villages such as Castelnou, I eventually parked my car under the shady plane trees in the main square at Céret. I had two very good reasons to wish to visit this bustling town set in the Vallée de la Tech. I wanted to visit the Musée d'Art Moderne, the Mecca of Cubism with works dedicated to the town of Céret by such famous names as Chagall, Picasso and Matisse, and so laudably kept in the beloved surroundings of the artists rather than added to some collection in a Paris museum. My other reason to stop was for the cherries. Not that it was the season for them in late September. I just wanted personal confirmation that they are the first cherries to ripen in France, that the first basket picked is sent to the President of France, and that every Easter the trees are ceremoniously blessed by the clergy followed by a semi-pagan ritual on the village streets. It was all confirmed by Jean, a fruit grower and *vigneron* with whom I shared a sturdy *casse-croûte des vendangeurs*.

I spent the day exploring the fertile valley and that night Jean's wife Josette gave us a sumptuous dinner of Catalan origin. We started with freshly picked black and white figs with thin slices of local raw ham. Then a dish of meatballs served with haricot beans, *Bolas de picolat*, and to finish, a sharp cherry tart made with that year's preserves.

Bolas de picolat

SPICY MEATBALLS WITH BEANS

MEATBALLS
500 g/1 lb freshly minced pork
200 g/7 oz freshly minced beef
2 eggs, beaten
3 garlic cloves, crushed
2 teaspoons finely chopped parsley
salt and pepper
flour

SAUCE
1 tablespoon olive oil
150 g/5 oz unsmoked bacon, cut into *lardons*
1 onion, finely chopped
4 small carrots, finely diced
bean stock
1 large fresh tomato, peeled and chopped
2 tablespoons tomato purée
200 g/7 oz green olives, pitted
2 tablespoons Cognac
a pinch of chili powder
salt and pepper (optional)

BEANS
500 g/1 lb dried haricot beans
1 large bouquet garni

SERVES 4

Soak the beans for 3 hours. Rinse and cook in plenty of boiling water with the bouquet garni until tender. Leave in the stock until the last minute.

Make the meatballs. In a mixing bowl combine the two meats with the beaten eggs, garlic, parsley, salt and pepper. Flour a wooden board and pour some flour into a saucer. Using the palms of your hands make regular-sized balls the size of a small egg. Roll each in flour and roll once more on the board to re-shape.

To make the sauce, heat the olive oil in a large cast iron or flameproof casserole. Sauté the bacon *lardons* until transparent. Remove from the pot and sauté the meatballs on all sides until golden-brown. Remove from the pot. Sauté the chopped onion and carrots, tossing well. Return the meatballs to the pot with the bacon. Pour enough bean stock over them to cover the meat and add the fresh tomato, tomato purée, olives, Cognac and chilli.

Season if necessary. Cover, reduce the heat and simmer for 1 hour.

Just before serving, drain the haricot beans from the remaining stock, add them to the casserole and simmer for a further 10–15 minutes, uncovered. Check the seasoning and serve at once with plenty of bread and a rich red wine.

Le casse-croûte des vendangeurs

THE GRAPE-PICKERS' BREAKFAST

◇

Boil a bulb of garlic with the skin on. Skin each clove and mash with pork or duck dripping, and plenty of salt and pepper. Spread on thick slices of bread and eat with a bunch of grapes . . . and a glass of red *vin de pays*.

Freshly picked haricot beans.

Opposite: A Roussillon farmyard.

—— 'The only way to eat anchovies . . .' ——

I left Céret before the sunrise en route to Port-Vendres and Collioure, the two main anchovy fishing ports of France. I had fond memories of the Côte Vermeille. Sadly it has now suffered from the benefits of tourism, and I found apartment blocks where I remembered vineyards and fields of pomegranate trees facing the sea.

But at that time of the morning everything was quiet and activity concentrated on the main industry of the area: the salting of fresh anchovies from the Golfe du Lion. I met Monsieur Desclaux on the quay at Port-Vendres where he was anxiously awaiting the return of the early morning catch.

From there we drove to the salting sheds in Collioure where women have been filleting anchovies daily for the past thirty years. I watched with fascination the dexterity of hands deeply chapped by the constant contact with brine. They were working with the concentration and assiduity of a first day.

At eleven o'clock, a bottle of Vin de Collioure was opened and Madame Desclaux arrived with a magnificently presented platter of *anchois de Collioure – hors-d'oeuvre*, with red peppers and hard-boiled eggs. 'La seule facon de goûter les anchois,' said Monsieur Desclaux as we started eating.

Above: Collioure – the harbour and old anchovy fishing boat.

Anchois de Collioure

ANCHOVY AND RED PEPPER SALAD

◇

Soak the salted anchovies for 2 hours in plenty of cold water. Scrape the skin off and divide into fillets. Grill a red pepper until the skin blisters and browns. Peel and cut into fine strips. Marinate for 2 hours in olive oil, salt and pepper.

Hard-boil 2 eggs. Finely chop a handful of fresh parsley and crush a large garlic clove.

To serve, arrange the anchovy fillets in a star shape on a large round serving platter. Place the strips of red pepper in between. Coarsely chop the hard-boiled eggs. Mix with the parsley and garlic and sprinkle all over the dish. Serve with a dash of olive oil.

Above: Salted anchovies.

Right: Filleted anchovies ready for bottling.

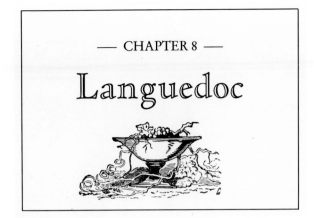

— CHAPTER 8 —
Languedoc

The Languedoc is Toulouse, Castelnaudary, Carcassonne and succulent *cassoulet*. The Languedoc is a mauve sunset on a salty lake around Sète and Montpellier and the clams and *moules* of Bouzigues. The Languedoc is also Nîmes, the great Roman city of France, and the famous *brandade de morue*, a smooth dish of salt cod.

These are some of the best-known aspects of the region, but there is also the rural north, towards the Cévennes mountains, where the stony fruit fields and vineyards are covered through spring and summer with the scented herbs of the *garrigue*. At the centre of the province lie two prolific valleys – of the Gard and Hérault rivers – producing peaches, melons and apricots and the earthy *vins du pays*. The clear waters of the Hérault flow away from the foothills into the Hérault region itself – a clandestine harbour of peace where fragrant woods of wild herbs and evergreen oaks hide medieval stone villages and crumbling farmsteads. There the hare eats rosemary and wild mint, the last olive trees of neighbouring Provence mingle with sweet chestnuts and medlar trees, the river trout is free to jump and, in the early autumn, the fruits gathered from country walks provide some very unusual dishes.

It was at a farm between the Cévennes and the more arid limestone *causses* that I tasted, for the first time, the *cornouille*, a red berry indigenous to the region. Once picked it had been spiced and kept to mature in an earthenware crock. It was then added, with a touch of vinegar, to a fricassee of chicken. The taste was tangy, mysterious, almost exotic, a fine example of local knowledge in the rural French kitchen. Here, hidden in those inland pocket, traditions have protected themselves

Fishing nets, Bouzigues.

from the erosion of old regional frontiers. Each area, each city seems to have its speciality, its natural nuances. Montpellier has its very own recipe for herb butter, Sète its very distinctive *soupe de poisson*, Toulouse its coarse garlic sausage – as well as the delicately candied violets used for the decoration of cakes throughout France. Whether one is in Nîmes or Narbonne makes a great difference in the preparation of escargots and, as far as the most famous dish of the region is concerned, the *cassoulet* – a warming dish of meat, poultry and haricot beans, cooked with wine and tomatoes – the recipe varies with every farm and village, from Carcassonne to Toulouse and Castelnaudary.

The traveller in search of culinary traditions could be forgiven if he chose to shy away from the flat littoral. There, the atrocious effects of modern-day architects have managed to mar the beauty of the wild and placid coastline. What was once a succession of salty lagoons from the Roussillon all the way to the Camargue is now a bleak playground for the holidaymakers.

But by the time I reached the backwater of Sète, in Bouzigues, the world of French regional traditions reappeared when I met with a group of ladies who seemed to have a great knowledge of how to prepare the whole range of shellfish found in the region . . .

── The Knitting Party ──

Bouzigues, September 29. Since I left Collioure I seem to have driven for hours through a soulless landscape of newly erected holiday resorts. Even the industrial site of Sète was welcome after such ugliness.

I am now on the other side of the Bassin de Thau, in the village of Bouzigues, one of the great shellfish centres of France.

Three old ladies have just sat down by me in the leafy square facing the oyster beds. One is taking her knitting out of a bag, the other two follow suit. Their accent denotes they are from the region . . . They must have a kitchen, they must do some cooking . . . I'll talk to them.

Bouzigues, September 29, one hour later. I have said my farewells, and, in my notebook I have local shellfish recipes from a lady who not only has a kitchen and knows how to cook but was for years a professional cook for a Parisian aristocrat.

These are a few of his favourite dishes.

Huitres gratinées de Bouzigues

—— BAKED OYSTERS ——

◇

Preheat the oven to 220°C/425°F/gas mark 7.

Choose large oysters. Open them and drain off the liquid. Into each one pour a little dry white wine and sprinkle with a touch of crushed garlic, plenty of chopped parsley and grated cheese. Place a knob of butter on each one and a sprinkling of breadcrumbs. Bake in the hot oven for 15 minutes. Serve at once.

Moules à la sauce verte

—— COLD MUSSELS WITH A HERB MAYONNAISE ——

◇

Choose large mussels. Wash and clean them thoroughly. Steam them open. Remove the top shell and lay them flat on a serving dish. Make a mayonnaise with one teaspoon strong mustard, a touch of garlic, one egg and one tablespoon finely chopped parsley. Spoon some mayonnaise over each mussel. Serve chilled as a first course.

Moules farcies

—— STUFFED MUSSELS ——

This is a good main course.

◇

32 large mussels
200 g/7 oz sausage-meat
2 garlic cloves, crushed
2 teaspoons finely chopped parsley
black pepper
3 tablespoons olive oil
300 ml/½ pint spicy tomato sauce *(see page 158)*
1 teaspoon dried thyme
boiled rice, to serve

—— SERVES 4 ——

Wash and clean the mussels thoroughly. Prise them open and drain well. Mix together the sausage-meat, garlic and parsley and season well with black pepper. Spoon some of the mixture inside each mussel. Tie each one with thread. Heat the oil in a deep frying pan and sauté the mussels on each side. Reduce the heat and leave to simmer gently, pan uncovered, for about 20–25 minutes, turning each mussel from time to time. Halfway through cooking sprinkle the thyme over the oil.

When the time is up, spoon off the excess oil. Pour the tomato sauce over the mussels and cook gently until the sauce is heated through and coats the shellfish. Serve with boiled rice.

Back street, Bouzigues.

The summer kitchen.

—— The Summer Kitchen ——

From Bouzigues I travelled to the Vallée de l'Hérault. I followed the river through an idyllic landscape of narrow wooded roads, with bridges so small they can only be crossed on foot, lonely country churches nestling in the foothills and always the soft sound of the meandering river and its deep-set tributaries such as the Buèges.

I could fully understand why Janine, a Normandy friend, went there on holiday one year, bought an old derelict house and never returned.

I found her in an ancient *mas*, a large farmhouse with courtyards so old the stones are shiny with the patina of wear, vaulted rooms with flagstone floors which keep cool even through the scorching summer months. There is so much space in this rambling property that Janine decided to have two kitchens. One – small, set in one of the turrets overlooking the vista – is the winter kitchen. In the summer, an open vaulted area at one corner of the middle courtyard is used. A stone sink, a built-in barbecue, a second-hand wood-covered *bistro* refrigerator and an old stove are the fittings of a very cool and shady *cuisine en plein air*.

We ate there shaded by exotic plants, the air scented with the heady perfume of the creeping jasmine and the purple bougainvillea.

Janine, who has now lived in the area for almost twenty years, has adopted the southern way of cooking, using lots of herbs gathered in the surrounding woods. We lunched off a fine green bean and cherry tomato salad tossed in a garlicky dressing with toasted pine nuts, followed by *loup de mer*, a firm white fish poached in a well-flavoured *court-bouillon* and served with a *beurre de Montpellier*. We finished with black figs and grapes, just picked, still covered with their natural powdery bloom.

That night, we ate a *ravien cévenol*, a salad made of mashed potatoes, *frisée* and walnuts. With it Janine served thin slices of raw ham and local dry sausage. We then indulged in a dish of garlicky *cèpes* brought by her neighbour that afternoon.

Beurre de Montpellier

— HERB BUTTER —

This butter may be used to garnish fish and grilled or cold meat. It is also excellent spread on light brown bread as a base for a sandwich.

◇

1 bunch watercress
3 large spinach leaves
a handful of parsley
a handful of chervil
a few tarragon leaves
a handful of chives
2 large gherkins, sliced
2 teaspoons capers
3 hard-boiled egg yolks
a touch of garlic
3 anchovy fillets
500 g/1 lb butter, at room temperature
a little lemon juice
black pepper

—————— MAKES ABOUT 600 G/1¼ LB ——————

Blanch the watercress, spinach and all the herbs in boiling water for 2 minutes. Drain and rinse under the cold tap, then drain again, squeezing out as much moisture as possible. Place in a mortar with the gherkins, capers, hard-boiled egg yolks, garlic and anchovies. If you must use a food processor or electric blender work quickly so not to bruise the greens. Pound into a thick dry paste. Now pound the butter into it, adding a little lemon juice and black pepper. Place in an earthenware storing jar and keep covered and refrigerated.

To serve with fish or grilled meat, dot fine slivers of the butter over and leave to melt naturally with the heat of the fish or meat. Accompany with a quarter of lemon.

The winter kitchen.

Ravien cévenol

— SALAD WITH MASHED POTATOES —

500 g/1 lb potatoes
1 *frisée* lettuce, finely chopped
20 walnut kernels
1 cooking apple, peeled and diced
3 celery sticks, diced
3 tablespoons walnut oil
1 tablespoon white wine vinegar
salt and pepper

—————— SERVES 4–6 ——————

Cook the potatoes and mash without the addition of any butter. In a large salad bowl place a layer of mashed potatoes, a layer of *frisée*, a layer of walnuts, a layer of apple, a layer of celery. Make a vinaigrette dressing with the remaining ingredients and pour over the salad without tossing.

Cèpes des Cévennes

— CÈPES COOKED IN OIL AND GARLIC —

500 g/1 lb wild mushrooms
2 tablespoons virgin olive oil
1 large garlic clove, crushed
1 tablespoon parsley, finely chopped
salt and pepper

—————— SERVES 6 ——————

Clean the *cèpes* thoroughly with plenty of kitchen paper and discard the earthy tips. Slice the heads and stems in half. Heat a good amount of virgin olive oil in a heavy frying pan (a copper pan is ideal). When hot, throw in the mushrooms, the crushed garlic clove, crushed, finely chopped parsley and salt and pepper. Toss well until the mushrooms are golden. Reduce the heat, cover the pan and leave to simmer very gently for 1 hour. Check the seasoning and serve with plenty of bread and a good southern red wine.

— CHAPTER 9 —

Provence

Between the Alps, the Mediterranean and the river Rhône lies the vast region of Provence. For centuries, like some priceless *objet d'art*, Provence has been borrowed, copied, misused, often stolen. If the Greeks, the Romans, the Popes and a variety of artists have left their mark in places such as Nîmes, Orange, Arles and Avignon, adding to or simply recording the superlative splendour of the natural landscape, the layman and the unwitting have, over several decades, too often tried to claim this rich, sunny, scented land as their glamorous playground.

Yet among these warm hills, these Roman or feudal treasures, the fierce blue sky and the soft ochre of the high-perched villages, those who were born and belong here carry on, unperturbed, with a seemingly timeless simplicity of lifestyle – that of the mountain shepherd, the fisherman, the farmer, the flower or fruit grower, the *vigneron*. It is above all the highly traditional way of life of the Provençal family, united in their attachment to the secular rites of the region. Through their love for the place and sheer hard work they all contribute to the cornucopia of Provence and its table.

Spring starts early in Provence and, on the plains and in the valleys, in fields screened by bamboos or cyprus trees for protection against the fierce *mistral* wind, the first fruit and vegetables of the season – and the first in France – come to full ripeness in early May. On the slopes of the surrounding hills and mountains, herbs such as thyme, *sarriette*, rosemary and sage start to spread their scented growth on the arid ground. Nothing is more tempting than the bold array of young vegetables on display at markets throughout

Provençal scenery.

Provence. There is garlic of course, plump ivory-coloured cloves which give an immediate southern flavour to a tomato sauce, or bite back when used generously in *aïoli* – a mayonnaise prepared to be eaten as a first course with a variety of lightly cooked vegetables, fish, shellfish and tiny *escargots*. These are cauliflowers, early purple artichokes, tender peas and asparagus, large spring onions, broad beans and unusual salad greens, but also strawberries, cherries mingling with bright waxy lemons, tangerines and four-seasons oranges. Later on, as summer comes, tomatoes, large aubergines and all kinds of indigenous courgettes such as the firm *violon de Nice* will be sliced, mixed with thick olive oil and simmered or baked into wonderful *gratins* known as *tians*. Spinach will be eaten with sardines or mixed with rice ready to enter the stuffing of exotic looking fish or larger-than-usual mussels or clams. Dish after dish of *ratatouille* will be prepared and often eaten cold as a first course. As accompaniments, the sculptured flat bread *fougasse*, rice from the Camargue fields and all kinds of freshly made pasta inspired by neighbouring Italy. To conclude the meal there will be juicy large peaches or freshly picked figs or table grapes.

If *bouillabaise*, the fabled fish soup of Marseille, *pan bagnat*, a flat bread roll oozing with crisp tuna or anchovy-flavoured *salad niçoise* and *soupe au pistou* are among the best known of Provençal sun-kissed dishes, there are plenty of others to be prepared according to the season or the weather. Fresh vegetables and fruit are a daily feature of the Provençal diet. Fish is often grilled with herbs having been marinated in olive oil and lemon juice.

Lamb, the staple meat of Provence is either grilled, baked or roasted, while rabbit and other game are richly prepared in wine sauces. In winter, soups are made with chestnuts or chick-peas and wonderful beef *daubes* simmer on the stove, still retaining the pungent taste of the Provençal summer when flavoured with tomatoes, wild mushrooms, green or black olives, anchovies and pieces of sun-dried orange peel. For even Provence claims its winters and its bad weather as I found out at the start of my trip there.

—— *La Veillée* at Charens ——

Late April was inclement in the Drôme valley. At Die, turbid water gushed at the foot of the ancient cathedral town. Heavy clouds masked the snowy summits ahead. The mountain climb to the lonely hamlet of Charens would take a while. I telephoned my shepherd friends to say I would be too late for dinner. 'Don't worry,' said Chantal, 'two newborn lambs are due tonight, it will be a long *veillée*. There is a *soupe* and a *pogne* made by my mother-in-law for supper. It is so cold, we will sit by the fire and drink home-made walnut wine.'

La veillée, a phrase I had not heard in years, means time spent quietly *en famille* around the fire between dinner and supper. Suddenly the fatigue of a day's drive vanished as I resumed the narrow and sinuous journey in full anticipation of retained tradition. When I arrived, the stone-built *bergerie* was in darkness. Through the tiny window I could see that the ceiling light had been lowered over the huge table. Around it, father and son were reading, the two women knitting. As I entered the room, I was met by the aroma of woodsmoke and the rich, yeasty fragrance of the large pastry *pogne* awaiting us on the table, an appetizing sight for a hungry traveller.

First came soup, a fresh vegetable *potage* of dandelions picked that afternoon on the mountain-side. It was soothing and deliciously refreshing – somehow my lunchtime snack of farm Reblochon and bread seemed a long way away.

While her husband poured the syrupy walnut wine, Chantal sliced the pastry. The golden sweet *brioche* was passed round. It was light and buttery with the unmistakable orange-flower flavour which is to be found in many pastries and confectioneries in the South.

My hosts explained the origins of the word *pogne*. It is a derivative from *pougna*, a local *patois* word for *poignée* or 'handful'. 'In the old days,' said the blue-eyed lavender grower father, 'mother used to bake the bread at home and a small handful of sugared leftover dough would be baked separately as an afternoon treat for us children.' Over more prosperous years, richer ingredients, such as butter, eggs, citrus peel or candied fruit were added.

The peaceful foursome went on discussing other culinary traditions of their area, recalling special dishes prepared for a wedding or a child's christening, all of it reflecting the uncomplicated simplicity of a life of near self-sufficiency.

Charens and its neighbouring hamlet of Haut Charens claim thirty inhabitants. The tiny community tucked away at a height of some 1,000 metres can only be reached by a narrow road. Although cars and communications have changed life drastically since eighty-year-old André was born there, the Lageaix family still follow the old traditions and make the best use of their natural seasonal surroundings.

In spring, after the rigours of the lambing season, sheep are led to graze on the aromatic slopes. There, the first tender shoots of wild dandelion and asparagus are picked; later, wild thyme, oregano and garlic.

Throughout the year, in the large kitchen, the heart of the farmhouse, while *daubes* of garlic-flavoured lamb or thyme-fed rabbit or hare simmer

on the ancient stove, Chantal and her mother-in-law Rachel prepare cakes, preserves and other confections from the first-gathered cherries, peaches, almonds and apricots of the summer, followed by chestnuts, walnuts and wild mushrooms in the autumn.

The abundance of vegetables means that vegetarian dishes play a great part in the daily diet at Charens. Simple soups flavoured with garden basil, *gratins* of courgettes or aubergines baked slowly in earthenware dishes with pungent olive oil, delicate vegetable and chanterelle omelettes. Goat's milk provides the daily cheese. Eaten fresh in the summer months, it is wrapped in cabbage leaves and aged from the autumn onwards, becoming more piquant by the day.

Drinks and liquors are also home-brewed for traditional celebrations: walnut wine for chilly nights, a light peach wine in the summer, a liquor

of wild raspberry true to the flavour of the mountain fruit. Lemons and oranges are added with lemonade to the local sparkling wine, Clairette de Die, making a thirst-quenching beverage for the hamlets' summer *fête* in August.

And then there is Christmas. The Christmas Eve supper is still the prerogative of Grand-mère. This meal is traditionally the same each year, a celebration of familial continuity. The Lageaix will start with a *soupe de crozet*, a freshly made chicken consommé in which small squares of light fresh pasta have been poached. To follow, a vegetarian dish of *cardons provençals*, a rich compote of cardoons (a vegetable of the thistle family eaten by all at Christmas in Provence) cream, garlic and anchovies. Then roast turkey studded with truffles from a cousin's woods near Valreas. To finish, gâteau and *croquets* made of walnuts and almonds, accompanied by sweet and potent walnut wine.

La soupe de printemps au pissenlit

SPRING DANDELION SOUP

1 large onion
6 small leeks
2 teaspoons olive oil
a large handful of lettuce leaves
a large handful of freshly picked dandelion leaves
1.5 litres/2½ pints water
500 g/1 lb spring carrots
100 g/4 oz young French turnips
1 bouquet garni
salt and pepper
a handful of parsley and chervil

SERVES 6

Slice the onion and leeks. Heat the olive oil in a large pot. Toss the onions and leeks in the oil until soft. Add the lettuce leaves and the dandelions. Cover with the water. Add the carrots and turnips cut into chunks, the bouquet garni, salt and pepper. Bring to the boil. Cover, reduce the heat and simmer for 45 minutes or until the carrots and turnips are tender.

Blend the soup in an electric blender. Transfer to a soup tureen and add the parsley and chervil, chopped very finely. Serve piping hot.

La soupe de crozet de Noël

CHRISTMAS CHICKEN SOUP

1 large boiling fowl
4 litres/9 pints water
salt and pepper
4 large carrots, scraped
3 turnips, topped and tailed
1 large onion peeled, studded with 2 cloves
2 garlic cloves, whole
1 bayleaf
2 thyme sprigs
2 celery sticks
4 large leeks, cleaned and upper green part removed
225 g/8 oz fresh lasagne
2 teaspoons dried tarragon
nutmeg

SERVES 8–10

Place the chicken in a large pot. Cover with the water. Bring quickly to the boil, skimming off any scum as it rises. Add 2 teaspoons salt. Surround the fowl with the carrots, turnips, onion, garlic, herbs and celery. Simmer for 2–3 hours or until the fowl breast and legs are tender. Bunch the leeks together and add them to the pan. Simmer for a further 45 minutes.

Remove the chicken and vegetables from the pan. Skim the fat from the surface of the *consommé* with a skimming spoon. Bring the *consommé* back to the boil until it reduces and thickens slightly.

Meanwhile, cut the lasagne and a large slice of chicken breast into even-sized squares. Add the pasta and the tarragon to the consommé. Cook in the stock until tender, then add the chicken pieces and a little grated nutmeg. Check the seasoning. Serve in shallow soup bowls.

Cardons de Noël à la provençale

BAKED GREENS IN CREAM,
WITH ANCHOVIES

If cardoons are difficult to find,
Swiss chard may be used instead.

◇

1 kg/2 lb cardoons or Swiss chard
salt and pepper
3 garlic cloves
1 large onion, studded with 1 clove
1 bouquet garni
6 anchovy fillets
2 teaspoons olive oil
milk
150 ml/5 fl oz *crème fraîche*

SERVES 6

Discard the leaves from the cardoons or chard and use only the ribs. Cut the ribs into regular chunks and boil them for 25 minutes in boiling salted water with 1 garlic clove, the onion studded with a clove and the bouquet garni. Drain well, reserving the cardoons but discarding the onion and bouquet garni.

Cut the anchovies into small pieces and sauté them in a large heavy based frying pan with the oil and the remaining garlic, crushed. Add the drained cardoons, cover with milk and simmer as gently as

Olive trees in a Provençal churchyard.

possible until the milk has evaporated. Just before serving, season with plenty of freshly ground black pepper and add the *crème fraîche*. Mix well with a wooden spoon while the cream warms up. Do not boil. Serve at once.

Gratin de courgettes de Charens

BAKED COURGETTES

Every housewife in Provence seems to have her very own recipe for *tian*, or *gratin* de courgettes. Some mix the courgettes with rice, some add peppers and browned onions, some add eggs, some use grated cheese, some don't. This version is one of Chantal's summer standbys. It is light and makes a delicious first course. Whatever the recipe, an earthenware dish (*le tian* in Provençal) is a must, for a genuine consistency in the finished dish.

◇

2 teaspoons olive oil
1 kg/2 lb courgettes, sliced but not peeled
1 large onion, sliced
2 garlic cloves, crushed
2 teaspoons dried thyme
salt and pepper
4 large tomatoes
2 teaspoons fresh shredded basil
4 teaspoons finely chopped parsley
150 ml/5 fl oz double cream
a little butter

SERVES 6

Preheat the oven to 220°C/425°F/gas mark 7.

Heat the oil in a frying pan and sauté the courgettes with the onion, 1 garlic clove, thyme, salt and pepper. Reduce the heat and fry gently for 20 minutes until the courgettes are soft, stirring from time to time.

Spoon the courgettes into the base of an earthenware dish. Peel the tomatoes, cut them into small cubes and dot them over the courgettes.

Make a *persillade* by mixing the remaining garlic clove with the basil and parsley. Pour the cream over the vegetables and sprinkle the *persillade* over the top. Dot with a few knobs of butter. Bake in the preheated oven for 20 minutes. Serve the *tian* immediately.

La pogne de Grand-mère

A SWEET BRIOCHE

15 g/½ oz fresh yeast
2 tablespoons lukewarm water
550 g/1 lb 2 oz plain flour
1 teaspoon salt
100 g/4 oz sugar
4 eggs
2 tablespoons milk
2 tablespoons orange-flower water
225 g/8 oz unsalted butter, softened
1 egg yolk mixed with a little milk, to glaze

SERVES 4–6

Crumble the yeast into the lukewarm water in a small bowl. Add 50 g/2 oz of the flour and mix to a sticky dough. Leave to rise in a warm place for 20 minutes.

Sift the remaining flour with the salt on to a large pastry board and make a well in the centre. Add the sugar, eggs, milk, orange-flower water and the yeast dough. Using the fingertips, mix the eggs with the other ingredients and then slowly draw in the flour. Lifting and slapping back the dough on to the board, knead until smooth. Now knead the butter into the dough, a little at a time.

Transfer to a lightly floured bowl, cover with a damp cloth and leave to prove at room temperature for 3 hours or until well risen.

Transfer the risen dough to a floured board, pat it and knock out the air. Shape it into a baba or savarin mould or non-stick tin.

Preheat the oven to 230°/450°F/gas mark 8.

Make a few incisions with a sharp knife over the surface of the *pogne*. Brush with the beaten egg and milk mixture.

Bake in the preheated oven for 15 minutes. Reduce the oven temperature to 180°C/350°F/gas mark 4 and continue baking for a further 30 minutes or until the top is golden-brown and the sides draw away from the tin. Transfer to a wire rack to cool. Eat cold or lukewarm.

Gâteau de noix

WALNUT CAKE

5 eggs
225 g/8 oz caster sugar
2 teaspoons baking powder
50 g/2 oz plain flour
50 g/2 oz cornflour
2 teaspoons strong black coffee
225 g/8 oz walnut kernels, chopped

SERVES 4–6

Preheat the oven to 180°C/350°F/gas mark 4.

Separate the eggs. Cream the yolks with the sugar until the mixture is pale and thick. Sift the baking powder, flour and cornflour into the egg mixture, mixing carefully. Fold in the coffee and chopped walnuts. Whisk the egg whites until very stiff and fold into the mixture. Pour into a greased round 23–25 cm/9–10 inch cake tin and bake in the preheated oven for 30–40 minutes or until the blade of a knife inserted into the centre of the cake comes out clean.

Croquets aux amandes

ALMOND BISCUITS

500 g/1 lb plain flour
225 g/8 oz caster sugar
4 eggs
2 teaspoons finely grated lemon rind
225 g/8 oz unpeeled almonds, chopped
1 egg yolk mixed with a little milk, to glaze

SERVES 6

Preheat the oven to 190°C/375°F/gas mark 5.

Sift the flour on to a board and make a well in the centre. Cream together the sugar and eggs until pale and thick. Pour into the well and draw in the flour with a metal spoon. Work in the lemon rind and the almonds.

Divide the dough into 2 balls. Starting from the centre, roll into 2 rectangles 2.5 cm/1 inch thick. Glaze with egg yolk mixed with milk. Bake in the preheated oven for 30–40 minutes until golden but not browned. Cool for a few minutes, then divide into squares and leave to cool completely on a wire rack.

Vin de noix de la Drôme

——— WALNUT WINE ———

Gather the walnuts at the end of June/early July
when they are well formed but still very green
and tender inside.

◇

**8 green walnuts
1 cinnamon stick
1 vanilla pod
200 g/7 oz caster sugar
1 litre/1¾ pints good strong red wine,
preferably from the region
125 ml/4 fl oz dark rum**

Wash and dry the walnuts and cut them into small
pieces. Place them in a large glass jar with the
cinnamon and vanilla pod sliced in half. Cover
with the sugar, wine and rum. Seal and leave to
macerate in a cool place for 40 days, shaking the jar
lightly from time to time to make sure the sugar
dissolves properly.

Strain the liquid through a fine filter into a
sterilized bottle, and cork. Keep in a cool place or a
cellar.

*Above: Preserves
cupboard at the
bergerie.*

*Right: Walnut wine for
winter nights.*

Vin de pêche de la Drôme

——— PEACH WINE ———

**6 juicy ripe peaches
1 litre/1¾ pints good dry white wine
200 ml/7 fl oz *eau-de-vie*
200 g/7 oz caster sugar**

Peel and halve the peaches. Poach the fruit in the
white wine for 20–30 minutes. Leave to macerate
overnight. Strain through a fine filter and add the
eau-de-vie and sugar. Bottle and cork. Drink
within a week, well chilled.

—— A Provençal Farm Kitchen ——

The rugged Route Napoléon took me almost all the way to the Var valley where my friend was expecting me. As I pushed open the double door leading to the Provençal kitchen, there she was, a trim, handsome woman busy preparing a batch of fresh pasta.

The kitchen was just as I had first seen it two years ago: the old enamelled wood-burning stove set among hand-painted Provençal tiles, the plain stone sink, the solid table in the middle of the room, a box of wood kept underneath ready to replenish the fire and, as before, masses of kitchen utensils hung everywhere. Pasta cutters, pastry cutters, mortars and pestles of all kinds, each one awaiting the preparation of a specific sauce. Old pans, new pans, copper pans, all orderly on hooks or shelves: the kitchen of a woman who loves cooking.

A cast iron pot was simmering on the stove. I immediately recognized the rich smell. 'You telephoned just in time,' said my friend. I had no need to lift the lid – she had prepared her much acclaimed *civet de lapin*. Suzanne is known among her friends to be the perfect French hostess. Give her ten minutes' warning and she will prepare a meal. Give her two hours and she will prepare a feast.

With the *civet* we would be served a dish called *inhocs sauce à la verte*, an old Provençal family recipe for light pasta. I watched her divide the dough into 4 portions, roll each one into a wafer-thin sheet and cut fine ribbons ready to be poached. Then she grated large amounts of cheese by hand on an ingenious grater which had belonged to a great-aunt. And finally out came the stone mortar and pestle to prepare the pasta sauce. Our conversation was never interrupted by the grinding noise of any modern electric gadget.

Taking down two of the many baskets hanging from the main beam, Suzanne invited me to join her in the garden. We gathered parsley, mint, young lettuce and roquette. Asking me to hold the flat basket, my friend climbed up the acacia tree and gently picked the heavily scented flowers. Another treat in store for dessert – the light acacia fritters I had so much loved during my last visit.

Honoré, Suzanne's husband, joined us in the kitchen, accolades were exchanged, the welcome *pastis* poured. With it, a bowl of tiny *niçois* olives picked at several stages of ripeness, green, brown, purple and black, all deliciously preserved in brine and spices.

The table was laid, wine fetched from the cellar – the earthy Vin du Var so true to the taste of its grapes. Suzanne's feast began.

First, a basket of crudités from the garden was served with a strong anchovy vinaigrette.

Above: Provençal farm kitchen.

Opposite: Fresh pasta to be served with civet de lapin.

Crudités à la sauce aux anchois

—— RAW VEGETABLES WITH ANCHOVY SAUCE ——

A traditional spring first course, this dish makes use
of the first-picked delicate vegetables of the garden.
Just wash the vegetables and arrange them in a basket.

◇

CRUDITÉS

The choice could be:

young broad beans, podded

tiny young purple artichokes, raw and quartered

small carrots, washed and tailed

radishes

celery

cauliflower florets

mushrooms

SAUCE AUX ANCHOIS (ANCHOVY SAUCE)

4 anchovy fillets

1 large spring onion, very finely chopped

1 large garlic clove, very finely chopped

4 parsley sprigs

a few *fines herbes*

5 tablespoons strong olive oil

1 tablespoon wine vinegar

pepper and a pinch of cayenne pepper

—— SERVES 4–6 ——

Pound together the anchovy fillets with the onion,
garlic and herbs. Make a vinaigrette by whisking
the oil into the vinegar. Add the anchovy mixture
and seasoning. Mix well. Serve with a fork or small
hand whisk in the jug or sauce-boat so that the
sauce can be whisked thoroughly before each
serving for the best flavour.

Le civet de lapin

—— RABBIT IN RED WINE ——

The last *tour de main* for a true *civet* is to thicken the
sauce with a little blood and the mashed liver. Any game
and poultry retailer will provide a small tub of the rabbit
blood when asked. If the idea does not appeal, thicken
the sauce with the liver mashed with a knob of butter
and a teaspoon of cornflour.

◇

1 rabbit

2 tablespoons olive oil

100 g/4 oz piece of bacon cut into small cubes (*lardons*)

2 onions, peeled and quartered

salt and pepper

1 glass Cognac

1 bottle good red wine

4 thyme sprigs

1 bayleaf

1 basil sprig

1 marjoram sprig

1 savory sprig

a pinch of mace

a pinch of nutmeg

1 clove

1 garlic clove, crushed

SAUCE

1 tablespoon Cognac

250 ml/8 fl oz rabbit blood

rabbit liver, mashed with a little butter

—— SERVES 6 ——

Mix the tablespoon of Cognac for the sauce with
the rabbit blood and keep refrigerated. Cut the
rabbit into 6–8 pieces. Heat the olive oil in a large
flameproof casserole. Sauté the rabbit on all sides
until brown. Lift the rabbit pieces from the pot
and keep aside while you sauté the bacon and
onions until lightly browned. Return the rabbit to
the casserole and season with pepper. Pour the
glass of Cognac over the meat and set alight away
from the heat. When the flames die down, cover
with the wine. Bring to the boil quickly and reduce
the heat to simmering point. Tie the herbs together
and add to the pot together with the spices and the
garlic. Mix well, cover and simmer gently for 1 hour
or until the rabbit pieces are tender.

Five minutes before serving, mash the rabbit
liver with the blood and Cognac, pour 2 tablespoons of the rabbit cooking liquid into the bowl

Left: Wild thyme and bayleaf – two main ingredients of Provençal cuisine.

Right: Shopping in the market at Nice – vegetables for a tian and a few pears to follow.

and mix thoroughly, preferably using a small hand whisk or a fork. Return to the casserole and stir constantly until the sauce thickens enough to coat the back of a spoon. Serve at once with fresh pasta.

Les inhocs

—— LOCAL PASTA ——

500 g/1 lb plain flour
1 duck egg
1 tablespoon vegetable oil
3 tablespoons lukewarm water
a pinch of salt
a pinch of black pepper
225 g/8 oz grated fresh Parmesan
and Gouda or Gruyère, mixed, to serve

—— SERVES 6 ——

Sift the flour into a large mixing bowl. Make a well in the centre. Whisk together the egg, oil and lukewarm water with salt and pepper. Pour into the well, then, using a spatula, draw the flour into the egg and mix until a dough is formed.

Transfer the dough to a floured board and using the heel of both hands knead for 10–15 minutes. Divide into 4 balls. Roll each one out from the centre as thinly as possible. Lay the sheets of pasta on a floured board and leave to dry for 30 minutes. Cut as thinly as possible into ribbons and poach for a few minutes in plenty of salted boiling water. Drain and serve with *Sauce à la verte (recipe follows)*.

Sauce à la verte de Grand-mère Chaix

—— MME CHAIX'S GREEN SAUCE ——

◇

a handful of parsley, chopped
2 mint leaves, chopped
1 garlic clove
1 teaspoon sea salt
1 tablespoon strong olive oil
1 tablespoon pasta cooking water
pepper

Pound the herbs in a mortar with the garlic. Add the salt, oil and water. Season with pepper. Serve on drained pasta with plenty of grated cheese.

Beignets de fleurs d'acacia

—— ACACIA FLOWER FRITTERS ——

This exotic-tasting dessert can be served only once a year when the acacia flowers are at their best. Elsewhere in Provence they are served in a savoury version as a vegetable. The batter needs to be very light and is therefore best made with water.

◇

100 g/4 oz plain flour
a pinch of salt
1 egg
1 teaspoon sunflower oil
water
sunflower oil for deep frying
12 acacia flowers
vanilla-flavoured sugar, to serve

—— SERVES 6 ——

Sift the flour and salt into a mixing bowl. Make a well in the centre and pour in the egg and oil. Whisk, adding water gradually, until the mixture is creamy.

Heat some very fresh sunflower oil in a deep frying pan. Place a small square of bread in the oil. When it rises to the surface the oil is hot enough to receive the fritters. Dip the flowers one by one in the batter and deep-fry quickly, making sure they do not brown too much.

Transfer to kitchen paper and sprinkle with plenty of vanilla-flavoured sugar.

—— Sunday Market in Nice ——

From the Var I went to the *pays niçois* where I paid a worthwhile visit to the Sunday market in Nice.

A Sunday morning visit to Nice is like a visit to the theatre. First take in the full glamour of the sea-front, the elegant Promenade des Anglais, the galaxy of celebrated hotels, the palm trees, the manicured dogs led by manicured beauties, and then go backstage. Whether through the narrow streets of the old town or along the vibrant market of the Cours Saleya, real people are enjoying a true French pastime – *le food shopping*.

I was there on May Day. The delicate aroma of lily of the valley filled the air. It is the custom throughout the whole of France to give a few stems of the frail white spring flower on that day. Not only was it on sale in the flower market but as I approached the other stalls, stems and larger bunches were to be seen everywhere.

Before I could witness the overwhelming variety of spring products, I was attracted by a corner of the square where small producers from nearby villages had humbly displayed the offerings from their market gardening efforts. I say 'humbly' because in the case of one old lady, all she had to sell were two eggs – one large duck egg and a very white and shiny bantam egg – a few bunches of wild thyme, a handful of early broad beans, a rabbit and a bunch of lily of the valley. Was it worth the trip? She certainly seemed to think so, if only for the animated chat she was having with the woman seated next to her.

I was still under the spell of this charming scene when a very official car carrying a very official-looking man went by. I learnt that he was the Mayor of Nice on his way to the May Day celebrations. I also learnt that he had just written a

Above: Spring storm – Nice.

cookery book, so horrified was he to have been served ersatz *salade niçoise* all over the world.

'*Vous comprenez,*' added the woman I seemed to have entered into conversation with, '*la vraie salade niçoise* should only be prepared with fresh *uncooked* vegetables. No potatoes, no cooked green beans. In fact it is at its best at this time of the year when artichokes are very tiny and small tender broad beans are just in season.'

We had walked across to a large stall, and because in this part of the world action speaks louder than words, she immediately opened a couple of broad bean pods and under the consenting eye of the stall-holder invited me to taste them with her. 'Mm, they are just right,' she said, and proceeded to eat the contents of another one. To my relief she bought a kilo.

By now the mid-morning sun was filtering through the surrounding buildings on to the market place, heightening the colours of the ripe vegetables. Shiny and enormous aubergines, tomatoes, some less ripe than others but firm, fleshy and flavoursome, crisp green courgettes, bunches of miniature purple artichoke were carefully chosen and disappeared into large baskets.

The stall-holders did not need to shout their wares. The discerning French housewife knew what she wanted for her kitchen.

More delicate vegetables and salads were to be found on the shady side of the market: sorrel, *blettes* – a kind of Swiss chard – fine wild asparagus, salsify, courgette flowers. These would either be filled with an appropriate light mixture or turned into fritters retaining the fresh taste of spring. And there was *mesclum* – some spelt it '*mesklum*', others '*mesclun*', a mixture of five different types of salad leaves, one of which was chickweed, a salad green introduced by the Romans. I ate some later on that day, tossed carefully in a vinaigrette made of farm olive oil and home-made red wine vinegar, a nutty and delicate mixture.

Further along, two ladies were sitting on either side of an old flat wood barrow laid simply with the fish their husbands had caught the previous night. A mother-of-pearl rainbow of *pageoline*, sardines and pink *pageot*, and others described as *soupa de pei*, a variety of small colourful fish awaiting the pot while garlic, onion, tomatoes and saffron are blended with rich olive oil and cognac to make a smooth soup stock.

—— Sunday Lunch in Nice ——

I walked on into the narrow streets of the old town, and as Sunday Mass was ending I joined the long queue outside the baker, determined to try the flat *fougasse* studded with anchovies or small black olives. With it I bought a portion of courgette tart and a square of freshly baked *pissaladière*, a *niçois* tart made with a thin bread dough base, brushed with *pissala*, a purée of salt, anchovy and sardine and covered with a thick coating of onions and garlic softened in olive oil, then dotted with olives and anchovies.

I ate these walking among the shady archways, stopping to look at fresh pasta shops, butchers selling intriguing black puddings made with spinach and rum, following Sunday shoppers through a labyrinth of ochre and terracotta alleys bearing colourful names such as L'Allée des Herbes. From opened windows came the clatter of pots and pans, the sizzling of oil being fried, the unmistakable smell of garlic . . . Sunday lunch was being pre-

pared in Nice. The following recipes for Sunday lunch were sampled and gathered during my time in Roquette-sur-Var.

Right: Vieux Nice.

La salade niçoise

CLASSIC NICE SALAD

Remember as a rule of thumb: no potato, no cooked vegetable, and, if anchovies are used, no tuna.

◇

1 50 g/2 oz can anchovy fillets
or 1 250 g/8 oz can tuna
4 eggs, hard-boiled
1 cucumber
1 large green pepper
1 red pepper
6 spring onions
6 large tomatoes
1 garlic clove
225 g/8 oz very young broad beans, podded (in season)
100 g/4 oz small Nice olives
1 teaspoon lemon juice
4 basil leaves
4 tablespoons virgin olive oil
salt and pepper

SERVES 6

Chop the anchovy fillets into small pieces or shred the tuna fish with a fork. Slice the hard-boiled eggs. Peel and slice the cucumber thinly. Slice the peppers discarding the seeds, and slice the spring onions. Slice the tomatoes.

Peel and halve the garlic clove. Rub the sides of a large salad bowl well with the garlic. Layer the anchovy or tuna, eggs and vegetable ingredients alternately in the bowl with the broad beans and olives. Season with plenty of pepper and a little salt. Prepare a vinaigrette with the lemon juice, torn basil and olive oil. Pour over the salad, toss lightly and serve chilled.

Gratin d'aubergines à la niçoise

BAKED AUBERGINES

This gratin is eaten cold as a first course during the summer months.

◇

6 large aubergines
salt and pepper
10 tomatoes
olive oil
6 tablespoons fine breadcrumbs
225 g/8 oz fresh parsley, finely chopped
6 fresh basil leaves, chopped
4 garlic cloves, crushed

SERVES 6

Slice the aubergines without peeling them. Sprinkle them with salt. Cover with a clean tea-towel and leave to sweat for 1 hour.

Preheat the oven to 220°C/425°F/gas mark 7. Peel, seed and slice the tomatoes. Rinse the aubergine slices and dry them with a cloth.

Grease an earthenware baking dish with plenty of fragrant olive oil. Line with a layer of aubergine, then a layer of the sliced tomatoes. Cover with a good quantity of *persillade* made by mixing together the breadcrumbs, parsley, basil and crushed garlic. Season with salt and pepper and repeat with a second, and even a third layer of vegetables, finishing with a layer of *persillade*. Spoon a good tablespoon of olive oil over the dish.

Bake in the preheated oven for 35–40 minutes. Leave to cool overnight.

A mother-of-pearl rainbow of Mediterranean fish.

Sardines à la niçoise

— BAKED SARDINES —

12 sardines
2 tablespoons olive oil
3 tablespoons breadcrumbs
a handful of small black olives
a handful of fresh parsley, chopped
1 garlic clove, crushed
juice of 1 lemon
salt and pepper

— SERVES 6 —

Preheat the oven to maximum.

Clean the sardines and discard the heads and scales. Wash well under the cold tap and pat dry with kitchen paper. Pour the olive oil into one bowl and place the breadcrumbs in another. Dip the sardines into the oil first, then coat with breadcrumbs. Lay them in an ovenproof dish.

Bake in the very hot oven for 20 minutes.

Five minutes before serving, scatter the olives and a *persillade* made by mixing the parsley and garlic, over the fish. Return to the oven for 5 minutes. Serve at once sprinkled with plenty of fresh lemon juice, salt and black pepper.

Fricassée d'agneau à la niçoise

— LAMB FRICASSEE —

1 tablespoon olive oil
1 kg/2 lb lamb fillet or boned leg of lamb, cubed
or 12 lean lamb cutlets
2 onions
4 tomatoes, peeled and chopped
2 garlic cloves
5 juniper berries
1 bouquet garni
150 ml/5 fl oz dry white wine
150 ml/5 fl oz warm water
1 teaspoon tomato purée
salt and pepper
50 g/2 oz pitted green olives

— SERVES 4–6 —

Heat the oil in a flameproof casserole and sauté the lamb on all sides until brown. Add the onions and sauté until transparent. Now add the tomatoes, crushed garlic, juniper berries and bouquet garni. Mix well. Cover with the wine and water mixed with the tomato purée. Season. Cover and reduce the heat to simmering point. Cook for 1 hour or until the lamb is tender. Add the olives 15 minutes before serving. Finish cooking uncovered. Check the seasoning and serve with steamed potatoes.

Poulet à la niçoise

— CHICKEN FRICASSEE —

1 large chicken
1 tarragon sprig
1 thyme sprig
1 bayleaf
3 sage leaves
1 tablespoon olive oil
100 g/4 oz unsmoked streaky bacon,
cut into cubes (*lardons*)
6 small pickling onions, peeled
2 garlic cloves
1 tomato, peeled and chopped
6 anchovy fillets
200 ml/7 fl oz white wine
150 ml/5 fl oz chicken stock
salt and pepper
100 g/4 oz pitted green and black olives, mixed
2 teaspoons capers
2 teaspoons orange juice

— SERVES 6 —

Cut the chicken into 6–8 pieces. Bunch all the herbs together into a bouquet garni. Heat the oil in a flameproof casserole and sauté the bacon *lardons* with the onions. Remove with a slotted spoon and set aside.

Now brown the chicken pieces on all sides, 2 at a time. Add the whole garlic cloves, tomato, anchovy fillets, wine, stock, bouquet garni and seasoning. Bring to the boil, cover, reduce heat and cook over low heat for 25 minutes. Add the olives and capers. Cook for a further 15 minutes or until the chicken is tender.

Transfer the chicken to a heated flameproof serving dish. Discard the bouquet garni and garlic from the sauce. Bring to the boil in the casserole and add the orange juice. Check seasoning. Spoon the onion and olive sauce over the chicken pieces.

Artichoke fields, Provence.

—— The Artichoke Fields ——

The Provençal artichoke is small, purple and so tender when young that many Southern people eat it raw in salads and hors d'oeuvres. In the Nice market bunches of the violet vegetable were simply laid on a long wooden bench. Paulette Cogiano and her husband had been up since dawn cutting and sizing. 'If you think this is a beautiful sight,' she said, 'you ought to come and look at the fields in the morning.' She has been an artichoke grower for forty-five years and eats them daily from mid-spring until late September, weather permitting.

Early the next morning, I followed her directions to the artichoke fields. At the end of the chalky lane, among acres of artichoke plants, stood a simple Provençal white house set in a garden of citrus trees, their waxy leaves and sun-gorged fruit shining in the morning sun. Only a dog and a large goose met me at the door. The owners were already at work. I joined them and during the hour which followed, Paulette never once stopped her tasks while at the same time feeding me mouth-watering recipes.

Artichauts aux petits pois

———— ARTICHOKES WITH PEAS ————

Three fresh spring vegetables simmered together make an ideal garnish for white roast meat, or are delicious served on their own.

◇

6 small purple artichokes
225 g/8 oz shelled fresh petits pois
2 teaspoons olive oil
6 outer lettuce leaves, shredded
6 spring onions, chopped
250 ml/8 fl oz water
salt and pepper
1 thyme sprig

———— SERVES 6 ————

Discard the stalks and bottom leaves from the artichokes. Blanch the artichokes for a few minutes. Drain well, upside down. Open up the vegetable with the fingertips and carefully scrape out the choke. Fill the centre with the raw peas.

Heat the oil in a flameproof casserole. Throw in the lettuce leaves and spring onions. Toss with a wooden spoon and cover with the water and seasoning. Place the artichokes standing upright in the pot. Add the thyme. Cover and simmer for 45 minutes, or until tender.

Omelette aux artichauts

———— ARTICHOKE OMELETTE ————

Generally eaten cold in Provence. Excellent for a picnic.

◇

6 small artichokes
1 tablespoon olive oil
9 eggs, beaten
salt and pepper

———— SERVES 6 ————

Cut off the tips of the artichoke leaves. Quarter each artichoke. Heat the oil in a frying pan and sauté the artichokes until tender. Pour the beaten eggs seasoned with salt and plenty of pepper over the artichokes and stir with a wooden spoon until the eggs are set and the omelette is golden-brown underneath.

Right: The proud artichoke grower, Paulette Cogliano.

Tian d'artichauts aux anchois

———— BAKED ARTICHOKES ————

A delicious gratin which can be eaten hot or cold.

◇

12 small artichokes
2 tablespoons olive oil
500 g/1 lb new potatoes, parboiled and sliced
4 anchovy fillets
salt and pepper
2 tomatoes, sliced
50 g/2 oz pitted black olives
2 garlic cloves, crushed
2 tablespoons chopped fresh parsley
olive oil

———— SERVES 6 ————

Preheat the oven to 200°C/400°F/gas mark 6.

Prepare and quarter the raw artichokes as in the previous recipe. Soften them in a little olive oil for about 10 minutes, while the potatoes are cooking. Chop the anchovies into small pieces.

Lightly grease the base of an earthenware baking dish. Cover with a thick layer of potatoes, and season. Then make a thick layer of quartered artichokes, and season again. Arrange the tomato slices and olives on top, together with the anchovy pieces. Mix the garlic and parsley together and scatter over the dish as a final layer. Spoon some olive oil over the top and bake in the preheated oven for 40 minutes.

Artichauts marinés

PICKLED ARTICHOKES

Served as an hors-d'oeuvre with a ripe tomato salad and
a few olives, this dish conveys the true flavour of the
South on one plate. For this recipe, the artichokes
should be really tiny so that the choke has not had
time to form.

◇

12 very small artichokes

MARINADE
450 ml/¾ pint water
1 large glass dry white wine
6 tablespoons olive oil
juice of 2 lemons
a pinch of salt
1 large garlic clove
1 teaspoon crushed black peppercorns
1 bouquet garni made of:
1 celery stick, 2 parsley sprigs, 1 fennel leaf,
1 bayleaf and 2 thyme sprigs

SERVES 6 OR MORE

Bring to the boil all the marinade ingredients
including the bouquet garni. Cut off the tips of the
artichoke leaves and arrange them side by side
in the marinade, away from the heat. Bring to the
boil, cover and reduce the heat. Cook until the
marinade has reduced by one-third. Transfer to an
earthenware dish. Keep cool until serving.

*A collection of olive
ladles, pestles and
mortars – each for a
different sauce.*

From the artichoke fields of the *pays niçois* to
Arles, the rice fields and an evening in the
Camargue . . .

Arles was exciting. In the space of one day of
food research in the vibrant museum city of
Provence I had the chance to view the original
painting of a pair of kippers by Van Gogh, separate
two women who started a heated argument in the
market place over a recipe for pumpkin, taste the
genuine *saucisson d'Arles,* receive a bunch of zinnia
from a real gypsy because I reminded him of a
woman he once loved, run red rice through my
fingers and spend an evening in a farmhouse in the
Camargue where my hosts recreated the atmosphere of one of Provencal author Alphonse
Daudet's short stories.

A salt lake in the Camargue.

—— An Evening in the Camargue ——

The last tourists had left. Dusk was setting over the Etang de Vaccares and in the mauve landscape between sky and salt lakes, pink flamingoes were turning the mud with their spatula-shaped bills. In the fields surrounding the *mas* – the Provencal farmstead – a soft wind teased the tufts of young rice. The Camargue was as wild and lonely as when I first discovered it thirty years ago.

My rice-grower host led me into the main stone-floored room where, over a large fire which had been lit with bundles of vineshoots, a spit was slowly turning. On it were chunks of eel strung together with spicy sausage. In the adjacent kitchen, his wife was pounding three large cloves of garlic in a mortar, ready for the *aïoli* sauce. The whole scene, some 120 years later, was an exact replica of a meal the local author Alphonse Daudet described as having shared with a *gardian*

and his wife in their humble hut in the Camargue. The setting I found myself in was certainly more opulent, but as in *Les Contes du Lundi* we 'ate *aïoli* with our eel' in a room lit mainly by firelight.

We started with an original salad made with three types of rice grown and processed by the family for the last two generations. The red rice, a new species, which took seven years to achieve, is organically grown at the foot of the Abbaye de Montjamour between Arles and Fontvieille. It is a useful addition to the cook's reportoire and, I have since discovered, looks splendid with any white fish.

The dessert was exceptional: the freshest of lemon tarts made with fruit picked from the garden that afternoon. Throughout the meal, an icy rosé wine which complemented all three dishes perfectly.

La salade de trois riz

— THREE-RICE SALAD —

If, unfortunately, red rice cannot be found,
use wild rice; the other varieties should be
brown rice and long-grain rice.

◇

**1 green pepper
1 red pepper
4 tablespoons olive oil
1 garlic clove, crushed
100 g/4 oz each type of rice
225 g/8 oz shelled petit pois
4 large ripe tomatoes
4 spring onions, sliced
2 teaspoons lemon juice
salt and pepper
50 g/2 oz black olives**

— SERVES 6 —

The day before, halve the peppers. Grill them until
the skin starts lifting and is quite black. Peel off the
skin. Cut the peppers into thin ribbons and leave
them to marinate overnight in 1 tablespoon of the
olive oil with the garlic.

A few hours before serving the salad, cook the
rice in salted boiling water following instructions
on each packet, rinse and drain well. Leave to cool.
Blanch the peas for 5 minutes in salted boiling
water, rinse under the cold tap, drain and leave to
cool. Peel, seed and slice the tomatoes.

Prepare the salad by mixing the rice, marinated
peppers and peas with the sliced tomatoes and
spring onions. Make a vinaigrette with the remaining oil and the lemon juice, season and spoon over
the rice salad. Mix well, dot the olives on the
surface and serve chilled.

Brochettes d'anguilles
à la gardiane

— GRILLED EEL —

**1.5 kg/3½ lb eel, skinned
1 glass dry white wine
2 teaspoons lemon juice
1 garlic clove, crushed
1 teaspoon crushed black peppercorns
9 pieces spicy sausage**

— SERVES 6 —

Cut the eel into even-sized chunks and place to
marinate in a deep dish with the white wine, lemon
juice, garlic and black pepper. Chill in the refrigerator for 3–4 hours.

Make the brochettes: alternate the chunks of
sausage and marinated eel on the skewers. Cook
over a barbecue fire or grill for 15–20 minutes,
until you are satisfied the eel has cooked through.
Remove the eel and sausage from the skewers and
serve with *Aïoli (recipe follows)* and bread.

Aïoli

— GARLIC MAYONNAISE —

To prepare the full-flavoured garlic mayonnaise of
Provence successfully, make sure that all the ingredients
are kept at room temperature for 1 hour beforehand.

◇

**10 garlic cloves
a little salt
¼ teaspoon finely ground black pepper
2 egg yolks
250 ml/8 fl oz olive oil
juice of 1 lemon
2 tablespoons lukewarm water**

— SERVES 6 —

Peel the garlic cloves. Chop them coarsely and
pound them in a mortar with the salt and pepper.
Work in the egg yolks. Add the olive oil drop by
drop, stirring all the time. When 4 tablespoons oil
have been added, stir in the lemon juice and water.
Continue adding more oil until the desired quantity
of mayonnaise has been obtained. The finished
product should be firmer than ordinary mayonnaise.

Tarte au citron provençale

— LEMON TART —

PASTRY
225 g/8 oz plain flour
a pinch of salt
1 egg
75 g/3 oz caster sugar
150 g/5 oz unsalted butter, softened
1 teaspoon finely grated lemon rind

FILLING
2 eggs
1 egg yolk
100 g/4 oz caster sugar
juice of 2 large lemons
100 g/4 oz unsalted butter, melted

— SERVES 6–8 —

Make the pastry 30 minutes before cooking time. Sift the flour and salt into a mixing bowl and make a well in the centre. Add the egg, sugar, butter and lemon rind. Using the fingertips, work the egg, sugar and butter together first, then gradually draw in the flour until a soft dough is formed. Form into a ball and chill for 30 minutes. Preheat the oven to 200°C/400°F/gas mark 6.

Roll out the pastry and use to line a greased and lightly floured 25 cm/10 inch tart tin. Prick the pastry case with a fork, cover the bottom and sides carefully with foil, weigh down with baking beans and bake in the preheated oven for 15 minutes until the pastry is set but not browned. Discard the foil and beans and leave to cool.

Meanwhile, prepare the filling. Using a hand or electric whisk, cream together the eggs and egg yolk with the sugar until creamy, then whisk in the lemon juice and the melted butter.

Place the tart tin on a baking sheet and pour the mixture into the pastry case. Bake in the preheated oven for 10 minutes, then lower the heat by opening the oven door until the thermostat reaches 180°C/350°F/gas mark 4. Bake for a further 20–25 minutes or until the filling is just set. Leave to cool for 1 hour before serving.

Left: at a Provençal farm.

Far left: Purple garlic – the true taste of southern cuisine.

The road to the olive farm.

—— The Road to the Olive Farm ——

My last taste of Provence took me through the vineyards of Châteauneuf-du-Pape, Gigondas and Séguret to the heights of Vaison-la-Romaine, then on to the road to the olive farm.

A long-haired girl was walking in front of me with the grace and self-assurance innate to Southern women. By her side, a blonde child struggled with an enormous bag. As I approached they smiled at me and, to the tune of their sunny accent, I learned that their father was an olive farmer and that they were taking a bag of black olives to neighbours.

Father was met a few metres away, tending the spring olive trees, pruning the young wood. 'When an olive tree is well pruned,' he said, 'a swallow can fly through it without folding her wings . . .' The moment which followed this wise comment was filled with an almost biblical silence. Was I to break it? I had to. I wanted to know more about the tree of peace and its wonderful fruit.

The children were told to take me to the farm where I would meet their mother. 'She knows a few recipes,' added Monsieur Charasse, 'and she will take you to the village olive press.' A week later, I was still with Simone Charasse, bread-deep in olive oil, exhausting the culinary possibilities of the *oliva* and the *oleum*. It started with our mid-morning collation, *la picoque* – large slices of *pain de campagne* rubbed with garlic and sea salt, quickly dipped in thick olive oil and eaten with handfuls of intensely flavoured black olives. With it, a chilled glass of rosé wine – a simple but felicitous snack at the end of a long morning walk.

Omelette paysanne de Nyons

OMELETTE WITH POTATOES,
BACON AND OLIVES

2 tablespoons olive oil
6 potatoes, thinly sliced
100 g/4 oz unsmoked bacon, cubed
1 onion, sliced
12 eggs
3 basil leaves
1 small garlic clove, crushed
100 g/4 oz pitted black olives, chopped
pepper

SERVES 6

Heat the olive oil in a large omelette pan. Sauté the sliced potatoes, bacon and onion, lower the heat and cook gently until the potatoes are tender. Meanwhile, beat the eggs in a bowl and add the torn basil leaves, garlic, olives and black pepper.

Bring the omelette pan back to medium heat and pour in the egg mixture, stirring with a flat wooden spatula, until the omelette is set and golden-brown underneath but still moist on top. Slide the omelette on to a heated serving plate and serve immediately with a salad of lettuce and dandelion leaves tossed in garlic vinaigrette.

La tapénade

SPICED OLIVE SPREAD

A spirited purée of olives, anchovies, tuna fish and capers, their flavours drawn together by the addition of olive oil and Cognac. It is served on toasted bread as an hors-d'oeuvre or added to certain dishes such as Simone's laudable rabbit fricassee *(see recipe below)*.

◇

225 g/8 oz pitted, fully ripened black olives
100 g/4 oz anchovy fillets
225 g/8 oz capers
100 g/4 oz canned tuna fish in oil, drained
1 tablespoon wholegrain mustard
5 tablespoons olive oil
1 tablespoon Cognac
freshly ground black pepper

SERVES 6

Using a mortar and pestle, pound the olives, anchovy fillets, capers and tuna to a fine paste. Add the mustard, then whisk in the olive oil, and finally the Cognac and plenty of pepper. Serve chilled with small slices of toasted French bread and a choice of raw vegetables.

Lapin à la tapénade

RABBIT FRICASSEE
WITH TAPENADE

1 large rabbit
1 tablespoon olive oil
12 pickling onions, peeled
3 garlic cloves
salt and pepper
4 tablespoons *Tapénade* (see previous recipe)
50 g/2 oz green olives
or 2 tablespoons chopped parsley, to garnish

MARINADE
1 glass dry white wine
4 tablespoons olive oil
fresh thyme and bayleaf

SERVES 6

Cut the rabbit into 8 pieces. Mix the marinade ingredients, add the rabbit and leave to marinate for 24 hours in a cool place, turning the pieces over at least once.

When the 24 hours are up dry the rabbit pieces with kitchen paper and reserve the marinade. Heat the oil in a flameproof casserole. First sauté the onions and garlic until golden but not browned. Set aside while you brown the rabbit pieces on all sides. Return the onions and garlic to the casserole and add the marinade and a pinch of salt and pepper (the later addition of the *tapénade* will add to the seasoning so be cautious). Cover the casserole and cook over low heat for 50–60 minutes or until the rabbit pieces are tender. If the sauce reduces too much add a little warm water.

To serve, transfer the rabbit pieces to a heated serving platter. Add the *tapénade* to the sauce in the casserole, stir well and check the seasoning. Bring just to the boil and spoon the sauce over the rabbit. Garnish with the olives or parsley.

Poitrine de veau farcie

—————— BREAST OF VEAL WITH OLIVE STUFFING ——————

A favoured dish in Provence, this is eaten cold with a green salad. The stuffing is extraordinary and so is the final result.

◇

Please note that you will need muslin, trussing thread, a large needle and some greaseproof paper!

1.5 kg/3 lb breast of veal

STUFFING
100 g/4 oz bread soaked in milk
225 g/8 oz streaky bacon, unsmoked, cubed
225 g/8 oz belly of pork, rindless, cubed
50 g/2 oz freshly grated Parmesan cheese
200 g/7 oz fresh shelled petits pois
50 g/2 oz pitted green olives
3 sage leaves, finely chopped
salt and pepper
4 eggs, hard-boiled

STOCK
1 small piece of marrow bone (middle cut)
2 large onions, peeled, one studded with a clove
2 carrots, scraped
1 leek, cleaned and trimmed
1 bouquet garni

a few black peppercorns
2 garlic cloves
2 glasses white wine
water
salt

——————— SERVES 6 ———————

Place the veal breast on a wooden board. Using the blade of a knife and your fingertips, open up the pocket it forms in the centre.

To make the stuffing, squeeze the milk out of the bread. Put the bread in a large mixing bowl with all the remaining ingredients for the stuffing, except the hard-boiled eggs, and mix by hand. Spoon the stuffing inside the meat. Line the hard-boiled eggs side by side in the middle. Using a large needle and trussing thread, sew the edges of the meat carefully together, making sure the stuffing is securely enclosed. Wrap the veal in a piece of greaseproof paper, then in a piece of muslin. Tie both ends and sew up the centre seam.

Put the veal parcel into a large pot and surround it with the stock ingredients, making sure it is completely covered with water. Bring quickly to the boil, then simmer for 3 hours.

Remove the veal and leave to cool in its wrapping. When cold, unwrap and serve carved into thick slices.

La picoque – a snack of bread, garlic, olives and olive oil.

Salade d'avocats aux olives

AVOCADO PEAR, GRAPEFRUIT
AND OLIVE SALAD

A very refreshing, unusual *hors d'oeuvre*

◇

3 large ripe avocado pears
juice of 1 lemon
1 large grapefruit
1 mild purple or white salad onion
50 g/2 oz pitted black olives
1 tablespoon top-quality olive oil
salt and pepper

— SERVES 6 —

Keep all the ingredients quite chilled and prepare the dish just before serving, as freshness is its essence. Halve the avocado pears, detach the flesh from the skin in one piece and divide into large cubes. Immediately squeeze the lemon juice over all the avocado pieces to prevent them from discolouring. Peel the grapefruit, divide into segments and cut each one in half.

Slice the onion. Layer the prepared ingredients alternately in a salad bowl, then add the olives, the oil and seasoning. Mix well without bruising the avocado pears and serve at once.

Salade chaude de haricots blancs aux olives

WARM SALAD OF OLIVES
AND HARICOT BEANS

500 g/1 lb fresh or dried white beans
1 bouquet garni
1 garlic clove
4 tablespoons olive oil
6 ripe firm tomatoes, chopped
1 sugar lump
1 tablespoon lemon juice
salt and pepper
50 g/2 oz pitted black olives, coarsely chopped
1 large salad onion, sliced

— SERVES 6 —

Soak the beans if dried. Cook the beans in boiling water with the bouquet garni and garlic until tender, adding salt towards the end of the cooking time. While the beans are cooking, heat 1 tablespoon of the oil in a non-stick pan, add the chopped tomatoes and the sugar lump. Cook until the tomatoes have almost caramelized.

Prepare a vinaigrette dressing with the remaining oil and the lemon juice, salt and pepper. When the beans are cooked, drain well and toss them in the dressing, with the caramelized tomatoes, the olives and the onion. Toss well and serve with thick slices of *pain de campagne*.

Pommes de terre aux olives

POTATOES SAUTEED WITH OLIVES

This dish of potatoes softened almost to a compote with herbs and black olives is so good that I recommend serving it as a vegetarian main course with a crisp Cos or Webb lettuce tossed in a light mustard and shallot dressing.

◇

1 kg/2 lb waxy new potatoes
2 tablespoons olive oil
8 large garlic cloves, whole
4 shallots, finely chopped
200 g/7 oz pitted black olives
1 teaspoon chopped tarragon
1 teaspoon chopped parsley
1 teaspoon thyme
4 basil leaves, chopped
pepper
a little water

— SERVES 4 AS A MAIN COURSE, —
6 AS AN ACCOMPANIMENT

Peel and cube the potatoes. Heat the oil in a large heavy-based sauté pan and sauté the potatoes, garlic and shallots until golden but not brown. Add the olives and herbs, season with pepper and mix well. Cover the pan and cook over a low heat for 10 minutes, stirring from time to time. Uncover the pan, add a small amount of water, and continue simmering, adding a little more water if necessary, until the potatoes are so soft they almost fall to pieces.

— CHAPTER 10 —

Corsica

'The originality of Corsican cuisine is a rich contribution to the unrivalled treasure of the gastronomy of France where each region guards its specialities. Corsica not only offers the splendour of its landscapes, the combined attraction of the sea and the mountain, it also offers the comfort and joy of its table.'   CURNONSKY

My visit to the 'Isle of Beauty' confirmed the revivalist writer Curnonsky's thoughts on the local cuisine. Not only was I amazed by the diversity of the diet but above all overwhelmed by the quality of the products.

How could it be otherwise when cattle are left free to graze the pastures and aromatic herbs of the *maquis,* when pigs feed off chestnuts and acorns, when fruit is left to ripen in the sun, when the sea is so pure that its catch is the envy of its continental neighbours, and when the thirsty traveller can quench his thirst with naturally pure water pouring from mountain rocks?

For centuries, the island was poor and divided. The fishermen lived off their catch, the mountain dwellers off produce grown on the rugged hills. Until recently the valley south of Bastia, which is now so fertile, was a malarial swamp. Wheat was unheard of and cornmeal and chestnut flour, ground by hand, were the only basics of a modest diet. But in the hard times of the past traditional recipes of the island were created by housewives eager to vary meals, including – after the yearly slaughter of the pig – the unusual *charcuterie* of Corsica. The meat was cured, sausages made and hung to dry or to smoke in the fireplace. Today they are still an exquisite speciality and mostly prepared in the traditional way.

Corsica – cattle and wild-life graze the aromatic herbs of the maquis.

The last century has seen the appearance of more modern cultivation on the island. Olive groves have been planted together with citrus groves, peach, apricot and almond orchards, vines and fields of southern vegetables such as peppers, pimentos, tomatoes and the recent successful transplantation of avocados and kiwi fruit. The crop is good and Corsican kiwi, avocado and clementine are to be found throughout the markets of the mainland.

To this day the Corsican cuisine remains totally original: like its people it is individual and sometimes fiery. Roast lamb and young goat meat are served with a spicy vinaigrette; tomato *coulis,* a thick tomato sauce, is often spiced with pimento before being served with a grilled fish. Exquisite omelettes are prepared with the local ewe's milk cheese, *brocciu,* and herbs gathered in the wild such as *nepita* (sweet marjoram) or wild mint. Chestnut flour is now very expensive and has become a minor luxury. Nonetheless chestnut cakes, pancakes and polenta are still made together with excellent ravioli and other pasta specialities.

Corsica was ruled by Italy for a long time, and as well as being famously the birthplace of Napoleon can also claim the Genovese Christopher Columbus, who was born in a back street of Calvi old town. The Italian influence is strongly reflected

in the dialect and in the cooking, and contributes greatly to the originality of the Corsican cuisine. The great Edouard de Pomiane used to say that names of Corsican dishes ring like music: *pebronata, nepita, falculle, pistacchini, torta, fiadone*.

'*Posa*' says your Corsican host as you enter his home. Accept his exceptional hospitality, a glass or two of Patriminio, one of the best-known fruity wines of the islands, and . . . '*a la vostra salute*', you have entered the Corsican way of life.

—— The Road to Vico ——

The white granite mountain village of Vico was to be my first port of call in Corsica. The slow drive from the historic port and citadel of Bastia revealed almost immediately the infinite diversity of the island. First I followed the fertile terraced gardens facing the Tyrrhenian Sea. At a farm I stopped to sample freshly picked avocado pears. Their taste and texture bear no resemblance to the imported variety. Like the fresh almond, hazelnut or walnut, there is no hint of oil at this stage, just the clean, individual taste of the fruit.

The next stage was a precarious mountain climb across the island, cutting through narrow escarpments and leaving well behind the littoral basking in the May sun. I drove slowly so as to appreciate the intoxicating plants of this natural herbarium known in Corsica as the *maquis*: absinth, rosemary, myrtle, juniper and fennel – each one used for some kind of culinary concoction.

Then through *u castagnetu*, the chestnut plantation whose fruit has always been part of the Corsican staple diet either as a vegetable or milled into a sweet flour for the preparation of numerous cakes and pastries. Finally to the top of the mountain still heavily covered with snow. There, a sign by a stonebuilt hut was advertising *dégustation* of smoked hams and pork products.

A few travellers had gathered around a basic table. I was invited to join them in a room darkened by smoke where the smell of cured meat mingled with the appetizing aroma of sausages grilling on the *spetu* (spit) inside the fireplace. A young woman was collecting the cooking juices on slices of bread. She was, she explained, cooking *figatelli* the traditional way. The *figatellu* is a very peppery sausage made of pork and offal. A winter favourite in mountain villages, it is eaten simply, in the fingers, as a warm sandwich, rich with the flavours of the meat and spices soaked into the thickly sliced bread. I resisted the offer of a second

glass of rosé wine, only too aware of the treacherous winding road I had to negotiate to finish my journey.

On leaving the forest at Eviza, the first glimpse of the Mediterranean horizon could be seen towards Porto and I started the slow descent through an array of bright soft petals, a solitary landscape broken only by a few hamlets and tiny churches. I finally reached the amphitheatrical setting of Vico, a large village built on three mountains overlooking the Liamone valley.

In the village square the atmosphere was very similar to any of the southern mainland villages I had left behind: a few cafés, a few food shops and a group of men seriously engaged in a game of *pétanque*. Just outside the village, on the terrace of a whitewashed pantile-roofed house, my distant relative, Ursule, who had returned a few years ago to her native village from the sophistication of a Paris *parfumerie*, could be seen totally involved with an open fire and the recreation of local cuisine.

Opposite: The square by the monastery at Vico, Corsica.

Below: Wild cyclamen, Corsica.

La Cena (The Dinner)

The wonderful climate means that a great deal of Corsican cooking and eating takes place outdoors. Most modern houses have a *'potager'*, an outdoor tiled fireplace, built on the terrace, where meat and fish can be grilled or cooked on the spit.

As I arrived, Ursule was basting the succulent meat which was to be my first taste of Corsican cuisine; roast *'cabri'* (kid). 'It is a dish prepared for very special occasions and honoured guests', she said. 'Tomorrow we'll have the pauper's soup!'

If Ursule's kitchen is too sophisticated to qualify as typically Corsican, her cooking is certainly very genuine. On the table a white tablecloth had been laid. In the centre a simple bouquet of four-season oranges and their flowers, freshly picked from the trees lining the drive. I was sent to the garden fountain to fetch a jug of crystal cold spring water and *la cena* commenced.

First a light spring soup made of young broad beans, peas and wild herbs, then the meat studded with slivers of garlic and parsley, crisped on the outside by constant basting with an unusual mixture of oil, vinegar and rosemary. With it, a simple dish of sautéed potatoes. For dessert the traditional Corsican cheese – Brocciu, served at its freshest stage with wild honey from the *maquis* and tiny green figs dried in the sun the previous summer. In the days that followed I was to learn so much more about this very versatile cheese named *le délice des dieux* ('the gods' delight') by the shepherds. But first the two main recipes of this excellent meal:

A suppa d'erbiglie

— SOUP WITH WILD HERBS —

1 kg/2 lb young broad beans in the pod
500 g/1 lb young peas in the pod
6 small new potatoes
2 large spring onions
1 large garlic clove
1 tomato, peeled
1 tablespoon olive oil
a handful of mixed herbs such as sorrel,
nettles, chard, a little basil or marjoram
1 litre/1¾ pints water
salt and pepper

— SERVES 4–6 —

Shell the broad beans and peas, peel and cube the potatoes, finely chop the onions and garlic. Chop the tomato. Heat the oil in a large saucepan and soften the onions and garlic in it until transparent. Add the broad beans, peas, potatoes and tomato. Cover with water, season and cook until all the vegetables are tender.

Chop the wild herbs as finely as possible, add to the soup and cook for a further 10 minutes. Season to taste. Serve unsieved with slices of bread lightly rubbed with oil and garlic.

Gigot de cabri à la broche

— SPIT-ROAST KID —

The same recipe can be used for a small leg of lamb.

◇

2 legs of *cabri* or a 2 kg/4 lb leg of lamb
2 garlic cloves
fresh parsley

FOR BASTING
3 tablespoons olive oil
1 tablespoon red wine vinegar
1 fresh rosemary sprig
salt and pepper

— SERVES 4–6 —

Prepare the basting mixture a few hours in advance by combining all the ingredients. Also two hours before cooking the meat, make small slashes all over it and insert slivers of garlic and a little parsley in each one.

Just before cooking, brush the surface of the meat with some of the prepared basting vinaigrette, season generously with pepper and a little salt, secure on the spit and cook for 20 minutes per 500 g/1 lb, basting very regularly with the vinaigrette. Carve and serve with sautéed potatoes.

Freshly picked orange, Corsica.

The Brocciu

If a large percentage of Corsican ewes' milk finds its way to the mainland for the preparation of Roquefort cheese, enough is certainly kept on the island for the making of various local cheeses and above all the fabled Brocciu.

The dairy I visited near Vico is on the ground floor of the shepherd's home, a square, stonebuilt house with large stone steps leading to the living quarters on the first floor where there is an outdoor terrace. The daily fresh batch of Brocciu was being made as I arrived. In the adjoining cellar row after row of the same cheese were drying and maturing.

I was particularly interested by the making of the fresh cheese as it is found in so many Corsican recipes. A large pail containing whey is warmed on a stove. When the whey reaches a temperature of 50°C/122°F, whole milk is then stirred in until the entire mixture reaches 75°C/167°F. At this stage a light curd forms on the surface and must be removed as diligently as possible with a skimming ladle and then transferred into small baskets and left to drain for a few hours. The fresh cheese is then ready to be eaten either with salt and pepper and a dash of olive oil, or as a dessert with sugar and honey.

Making the daily batch of Brocciu.

The terrace over the dairy.

La Cullazione

I had been told that the affability of the Corsican shepherd is legendary. It goes back to the days when shepherds used to spend lonely months in the mountains looking after their flock. Then the traveller was always welcome. I was, therefore, not too surprised when Jeannot, the shepherd, invited me to join his wife Marie and their young children for *la cullazione* – their mid-morning snack. The morning goats' milk had been boiled and placed on the table in an earthenware jug, together with a jug of fresh coffee. Marie was slicing a custardy mixture from a large baking dish. It was the *fiadone*, a lemony cooked cheesecake made with fresh Brocciu. While devouring my share I flipped through the pages of a well-used family recipe scrapbook in which were listed mouthwatering Brocciu recipes. Although I stayed long enough on the island to cook and sample the real thing, on my return I found that a good substitute for Brocciu is a firm, fresh Ricotta cheese. Here is a selection of The Brocciu recipes I found – from omelettes as a first course to cheesecake desserts.

Omelette au brocciu et à la nepita

—— CHEESE OMELETTE WITH SWEET MARJORAM ——

4 tablespoons Brocciu or Ricotta
salt
a handful of freshly gathered marjoram
4 large eggs
1 tablespoon olive oil

———————— SERVES 4 ————————

Roughly mash the cheese, salt and chopped herb with a fork. Add to the beaten eggs. Heat the olive oil in a 20 cm/8 inch omelette pan. Pour in the mixture, tilting the pan on all sides until the omelette is just set. Serve at once.

Omelette au brocciu et à la menthe

Proceed as above using mint in place of marjoram. If available, wild mint is best.

Petits artichauts et pommes de terre farcis au brocciu

———— ARTICHOKES AND POTATOES ————
WITH BROCCIU FILLING

A deliciously satisfying vegetarian dish.

◇

6 small purple artichokes
6 good-sized new potatoes
8 tablespoons Brocciu or Ricotta
2 eggs, beaten
salt and pepper
a little flour
1 large onion
2 garlic cloves
2 tablespoons olive oil
2 teaspoons tomato purée

———————— SERVES 6 ————————

Using scissors, trim the top of the artichoke leaves, push the middle open with the fingertips and discard the small choke, leaving enough space for the stuffing. Peel the potatoes and using a sharp knife make a cavity in each one.

Mash the cheese with the beaten eggs, salt and pepper. Spoon this mixture inside each vegetable, packing it in well with the back of the spoon.

Sprinkle a little flour on the surface of the cheese stuffing. Chop the onion and garlic as finely as possible.

Heat the oil in a flameproof shallow dish that will accommodate all the vegetables. First sauté them, floured side down, and as soon as they have taken colour turn them round so that they all cook with the stuffing upwards. Add the finely chopped onions and garlic to the dish and let them colour slightly. Then add the tomato purée diluted in a large cup of warm water. Cover and simmer gently until the potatoes are tender. Add a little water if the sauce reduces too much. Check the seasoning. Serve straight from the dish with large slices of country bread.

Les ravioli au brocciu

———————— CORSICAN-STYLE RAVIOLI ————————

The handwritten recipe read: *Les ravioli de la Maman Colonna.* Underneath: *Ingredients for 59 ravioli* – a puzzling number, but they are so delicate one could be quite tempted to make it 60!

◇

500g/1 lb plain flour
a pinch of salt
6 eggs
Parmesan cheese, for layering

FILLING
500 g/1 lb Swiss chard or spinach
6–8 fresh sage leaves
salt and pepper
350 g/12 oz Brocciu or Ricotta

———————— SERVES 6 ————————

First make the filling. Cook the greens and sage in salted water, squeeze out all the moisture and chop finely. Leave to cool, then mix with the cheese.

To make the pasta, sift the flour and salt on to a wooden board, make a well in the centre and break in the eggs. Using the fingers, draw the flour into the eggs and mix well until a dough is formed.

Lightly flour the board again and start kneading the dough with the palm of the hand, stretching and pulling it as much as possible. This operation should take between 10 and 15 minutes.

Divide the dough into 4 pieces. Starting at the centre, roll each one with a rolling pin into very thin rectangular sheets of the same size.

Lay 2 sheets of dough on the floured board. Place teaspoons of filling at regular intervals (roughly 5 cm/2 inches) over the surface. Using a pastry brush, moisten with the water around each portion of filling. Cover with another sheet of dough and press the edges together firmly around the filling. Using a pastry wheel or a sharp knife, cut the ravioli into squares.

Lower into a large pan containing plenty of salted boiling water and cook for 6 minutes until the cooked ravioli rise in the pan. Lift out of the water with a slotted spoon. Layer the ravioli in a shallow baking dish with plenty of freshly grated Parmesan. Pour over 2–4 serving spoons of Stufatu sauce (*see page 150*). Serve at once in shallow warm plates.

Making bastelle.

Les bastelle au brocciu

PASTIES FILLED WITH VEGETABLES, ———
HERBS AND CHEESE

Bastelle used to be eaten on Saturdays when they were cooked in the village bread oven at the end of the bread batch. This recipe comes from the Colonna family.

◇

PASTRY
12 heaped tablespoons plain flour
a large pinch of salt
1 tablespoon lard
6 tablespoons vegetable oil
5 tablespoons iced water

FIRST FILLING
500 g/1 lb Swiss chard or spinach
a handful of sorrel
1 tablespoon olive oil
1 onion, finely chopped
salt and pepper
500 g/1 lb Brocciu or Ricotta

SECOND FILLING
1 tablespoon olive oil
1 onion, finely chopped
a little crushed garlic
500 g/1 lb courgettes, sliced
a little fresh marjoram or oregano
salt and pepper
500 g/1 lb Brocciu or Ricotta

——————— MAKES 12 ———————

To make the pastry, sift the flour and salt into a large mixing bowl. Make a well in the centre. Add the lard cut into small cubes, then add the oil. With a spoon work the flour and fat together. Add enough water to make a soft dough. Transfer the dough to a floured board and knead for a while with the hands until light and elastic. Cover and leave in a cool place for 2 hours.

For the first filling, cook the chard or spinach with the sorrel in salted water. Drain, squeeze out the excess moisture and chop roughly. Heat the oil in a frying pan, add the greens and onion and stir until the onion is softened. Leave to cool, season generously and mix with the cheese.

For the second filling, heat the oil in a frying pan and stir in the onion, garlic, courgettes and herbs. Reduce the heat and cook until quite tender. Leave to cool, season well and mix with the cheese.

Preheat the oven to 220°C/425°F/gas mark 7.

Roll out the pastry on a floured board. Using a small salad bowl or 15 cm/6 inch cheese or dessert plate, and a pastry wheel divide the pastry into regular circles. Spoon some filling into the middle of each. Brush the pastry edge with a little water, fold the pastry in half and press the edges firmly together. Brush a little oil over each pasty, place on a baking sheet and bake in the preheated oven for 30 minutes. Serve lukewarm, or cold.

La fiadone

— LEMON CHEESECAKE —

4 eggs
4 tablespoons caster sugar
500 g/1 lb Brocciu or Ricotta
grated rind of 1 large lemon

— SERVES 4–6 —

Preheat the oven to 190°C/375°F/gas mark 5.

Separate the eggs and beat the yolks with the sugar until pale and creamy. Add the mashed cheese and the lemon rind. Whisk the egg whites until stiff and fold into the mixture.

Transfer the mixture to a buttered baking dish and bake in the preheated oven for 20–30 minutes until the top is puffed up and golden-brown. Leave to cool slightly or eat cold.

La papaccioli

— FRAGRANT CHEESECAKE —

Deliciously scented with Cognac, caramel and orange.

◇

175 g/6 oz caster sugar
500 g/1 lb Brocciu or Ricotta
4 egg yolks
grated rind of 1 orange
2 teaspoons Cognac
2 egg whites

— SERVES 4–6 —

Preheat the oven to 160°C/325°F, gas mark 3.

To make the caramel, melt half the sugar in a small saucepan with a little water. Cook until

golden-brown. Pour the caramel into a 1.2 litre/ 2 pint soufflé dish, tilting on all sides until the base of the dish is covered with caramel. Leave to cool slightly.

Mash the cheese well with a fork. Add the egg yolks one by one, then the remaining sugar. Mix well. Now add the orange rind and Cognac and finally fold in the whisked egg whites.

Transfer the mixture to the prepared soufflé dish and stand the dish in a bain-marie of warm water which should come halfway up the sides of the dish. Bake in the preheated oven for 40 minutes until the blade of a knife inserted in to the mixture comes out clean. Leave to cool in a cold place and serve when cold, but avoid refrigerating as this would impair the texture.

Les falculelle

—— CHEESECAKE WITH CHESTNUT LEAVES ——

To finish, an amusing recipe to make in the autumn after gathering chestnuts. The chestnut leaves curl up during baking to surround the cheese mixture. The result is a most attractive dessert.

◇

500 g/1 lb Brocciu or Ricotta
6 eggs
225 g/8 oz caster sugar
50 g/2 oz white flour
grated rind of 1 lemon
24 chestnut leaves
1 egg yolk, to glaze

—— SERVES 6 OR MORE ——

Place all the ingredients except the chestnut leaves and the egg yolk in a food processor and work until the mixture is perfectly smooth and homogeneous. Leave to rest in a cool place for 30 minutes.

Preheat the oven to 220°C/425°F, gas mark 7.

Spoon some of the cheese into the centre of each leaf. Place on a baking sheet and bake in the preheated oven for 10 minutes, then brush each cake with a little beaten egg yolk. Return to the oven for a further 5 minutes. Leave to cool. Serve with black coffee.

A Corsican picnic: bastelle, fiadone and home-grown olives.

Le Stufatu

The Corsicans eat a great deal of pasta: lasagne, ravioli, cannelloni, an obvious reminder of the island's long Italian association before being united with France in 1768. Lasagne are often cut very thin and added to thick soups, the traditional evening meal. Ravioli are mostly filled with herbs or vegetables; cannelloni with a pork mixture.

In Vico, the pasta speciality is the *macaronade au stufatu*, a dish originally prepared for wedding days when large families were all united. Still the pride of the Vico housewife, it is more or less a beef *estouffade*, cubes of beef simmered gently in a sauce of red wine and herbs. What I found extraordinary was that it does not seem to be cooked for its quality as a good beef dish but for the sauce it will provide for pasta. Hence I suppose, *macaronade au stufatu*, rather than *stufatu aux macaroni*.

This dish is tremendously filling and therefore does not feature on menus during the hot summer months. I watched its preparation and learned how to make the Corsican meat sauce. Most kinds of meat can be used, and I find it a wonderful stand-by. It is light, varies in flavour according to the main ingredient used and, above all, is so easy to remember. During my stay I sampled a fricassee of lamb cutlets, veal *paupiettes*, lamb's liver, stuffed artichokes and potatoes and meatballs all cooked in the same sauce. Each time I promised myself that I would recreate the dish at a later stage.

The stufatu pot.

Le stufatu

CORSICAN MEAT SAUCE

It would seem that red wine is always used regardless of whether red or white meat is being cooked. The secret of this sauce is above all the care taken to chop onions or shallots and the garlic cloves as finely as possible. It usually means that by the time the dish is cooked the onions and garlic have literally melted into the sauce, creating a natural thickening with the meat stock. Do not cut corners by using a food processor for the chopping – too much moisture comes out of the vegetables and they do not sauté so successfully.

◇

2 onions or 4 purple shallots
(called *échalotes grises* in France)
2 garlic cloves
1 kg/2 lb meat
1 tablespoon olive oil
1 teaspoon tomato purée
200 ml/7 fl oz red wine
1 bayleaf
salt and pepper

— SERVES 6 —

Chop the onions or shallots and garlic very finely. Brown the meat on all sides in the hot olive oil in a flameproof casserole. Using a slotted spoon, remove the meat and reserve while you lightly

brown the onion or shallots and garlic. Make sure they do not colour too much or the sauce will be bitter. Add the tomato purée diluted in the red wine to the casserole, and mix well, then return the meat. Add 2 glasses of warm water, the bayleaf and seasoning. Simmer, covered for 2–3 hours or until the meat is very tender. A little more water may be added during cooking if the sauce reduces too much.

La macaronade de Vico au stufatu

MACARONI WITH RICH MEAT SAUCE

SAUCE

1 kg/2 lb lean, well-hung chuck steak
225 g/8 oz raw country ham, cubed,
or cured smoked sausages or smoked bacon, cubed
1 tablespoon olive oil
2 large onions or 4 shallots, finely chopped
2 garlic cloves, finely chopped
1 teaspoon tomato purée
200 ml/7 fl oz red wine
salt and pepper
1 bayleaf
a pinch of rosemary
1 clove
a handful of pitted green olives (optional)

SERVES 6

As described in the previous recipe, brown the beef on all sides with the ham, sausage or bacon in the oil. Then add the finely chopped onions or shallots and the garlic. Brown lightly, then add the tomato purée diluted in the red wine. Cover with warm water and add the seasoning and herbs. Simmer gently for 2–3 hours or until the meat is very tender and enough sauce remains to moisten the macaroni dish (*see following recipe*). Add more water during cooking if the sauce reduces too much. Add the olives, if used, to the dish 30 minutes before serving.

Macaronade

MACARONI PIE

This is the macaroni dish prepared with the *stufatu* sauce and encased inside wafer-thin pastry. It comes out as a pie and a slice of *macaronade* is served per person with a little meat on the side. In some households the macaroni dish is eaten first, and the meat served afterwards with crisp lettuce tossed in a garlicky olive oil dressing.

◇

PASTRY

12 heaped tablespoons white flour
a pinch of salt
1 tablespoon soft lard
6 tablespoons vegetable oil
5 tablespoons iced water

MACARONI

500 g/1 lb macaroni
1 litre/1¾ pints salted water per 100 g/4 oz pasta
Stufatu sauce (*see previous recipe*)
225 g/8 oz grated hard cheese,
including Parmesan
freshly ground black pepper

SERVES 0

To make the pastry, sift the flour and salt into a large mixing bowl. Make a well in the centre. Add the lard cut into small cubes and the oil. Using a spoon, work the fat into the flour, adding enough water to make a soft dough. Keep in a cool place, covered, for 1 hour.

Boil the macaroni in boiling water until cooked *al dente* (6–8 minutes). Drain.

Preheat the oven to 220°C/425°F/gas mark 7.

Roll the pastry out as thinly as possible. Line the base and sides of a 1.75 litre/3 pint soufflé dish with two-thirds of the rolled pastry, making sure that it overlaps the top of the dish slightly. Spoon the drained macaroni into the dish. Add a large spoonful of sauce and a good sprinkling of cheese to each layer of pasta. Make sure that the final result is quite moist.

Roll the remaining pastry into a round lid and use to cover the dish. Press firmly with the overlapping pastry, to seal the edges. Bake in the preheated oven for 20 minutes until the pastry is cooked and crisp to the touch. Leave to cool slightly, then carefully unmould. Serve cut into slices.

A Walk in the Mountains. A Man's Kitchen

It had started as a wild herb picking expedition, a spring walk in the mountains. Within hours it became an adventure and a unique opportunity to discover the other aspect of Corsica – vibrant, receptive and welcoming but also secretive, hidden and defensive.

Although a car had gone by loaded with baskets of provisions on the back seat, nothing seemed to indicate that at the end of a long winding mountain track we would find a village. And yet there it was, clinging like an eagle's nest to the mountain slope. As we approached, the sounds which came from among the twenty or so roofs confirmed that the village was living and not one of Corsica's many abandoned communities.

Tired by the walk and terribly thirsty, I knocked at the first door to ask for water, which seem to start all the village dogs barking. A child came to the door, too busy digging his teeth into an enormous portion of fruit cake to ask any questions. From the depths of what looked like a huge kitchen a woman dressed in black with a long black scarf on her head spoke to the child in Corsican. Was she shy, or startled by the unexpected visitor? Her manner was dismissive. She indicated that I should stay on the doorstep. The child ran up a small stepped alleyway and within seconds reappeared surrounded by a herd of other urchins and with them, a jovial, open-faced, grey-haired man who introduced himself as Toussaint, a Corsican Christian name. After a brief exchange with the woman he led us to his house at the centre of the village. Nearby on a tiny square stood the communal bread oven, *u fornu*, still used every Saturday for the weekly bake.

We crossed a vegetable garden filled with herbs and lemon trees and climbed a few geranium-clad steps to *la sala*, the main room of Toussaint's home. *'Siate e ben' venutti'*, he said, pointing to two antique chairs on either side of the fireplace. As a first golden rule of Corsican hospitality, wine and water were immediately brought up from the cellar below. Glasses were raised and Toussaint explained that he lived on his own in this ancestral home. Could we please do him the honour of staying for lunch? Today it was wild boar cutlets cooked in red wine. An enthusiastic, extrovert man, he walked towards the fireplace in which the large cast iron pan, *la pignatta,* was hung. He lifted the lid and the delicious aroma made it easy to accept his offer.

The table was laid and potatoes added to the pan. The room was simple. A long bench and a few chairs on either side of a massive table, a doughbin in which the bread was kept, a cupboard where crockery and glasses were neatly arranged were, with the chairs on which we sat, the only pieces of furniture. Pieces of *coppa* and *migisca*, cured pork specialities, were hanging from the beam leading to the stairs. And beneath, the framed sepia picture of an ancestor. He looked magnificent with a large hat, a scarf knotted on his neck, a kind of cape hung on the left shoulder, a gun folded across his chest. On the opposite wall, severe against the whitewash, a rack on which eight guns were laid. 'Do you use any of those for shooting the boar?' I asked. 'No, for Frenchmen', he said. I still don't know whether he was joking.

We started with herby courgette fritters, then the wild boar and homegrown new potatoes richly impregnated with red wine sauce. We finished with fresh Brocciu and homemade ratafia of Morello cherries.

The excellence of the meal was explained by the fact that our friend had been a chef in the merchant navy for many years, but the felicity of the day was the product of pure Corsican conviviality.

Left: Sampling Grand-mère's cake.

Opposite: Spring in the mountains, Corsica.

Ragoût de sanglier au vin rouge

—— BOAR IN RED WINE ——

Boar is now available at specialist butchers,
but this recipe can also be made with venison.

◇

12 boar cutlets or diced cubes of meat
2 onions, sliced
1 tablespoon olive oil
300 ml/½ pint rich red wine
1 garlic clove
salt and pepper
a pinch of chilli pepper
1 teaspoon tomato purée diluted in a glass of water
6 medium new potatoes

MARINADE
2 glasses red wine
1 bayleaf
1 thyme sprig
1 onion

—— SERVES 6 ——

Mix the ingredients for the marinade in an earthenware dish, add the meat and leave to marinate
overnight. The following day, dry the meat with
kitchen paper. Discard the marinade.

Brown the meat on all sides with the onions in
the oil in a flameproof casserole. Add the wine,
garlic, salt, pepper and chilli. Now add the water
and tomato purée. Cover and simmer gently over
low heat for about 2 hours or until tender.

Boil the potatoes in their skins for 15 minutes.
Peel them and add them to the ragoût 30 minutes
before serving time.

The man's kitchen.

Les fritelles de courgettes

—— COURGETTE FRITTERS ——

225 g/8 oz plain flour
2 egg yolks
1 tablespoon olive oil
water
6 courgettes
2 young spring onions
3 mint leaves
salt and pepper
1 egg white
olive oil or sunflower oil, for frying

—— MAKES 12 ——

Prepare the batter. Place the flour in a mixing
bowl, make a well in the centre and add the egg
yolks and oil. Mix well. Add enough water to
obtain a thick batter.

Cut the courgettes into julienne-style sticks.
Finely chop the spring onions including the green
stems with the mint leaves. Add to the batter,
mixing well and season with salt and black pepper.
Whisk the egg white until stiff and fold in. Heat
1.75 litres/3 pints of oil in a deep fryer. Add a small
cube of bread to the oil; when it comes to the
surface the oil is hot enough. Lower tablespoons of
the mixture into the hot oil. The fritters are cooked
when they are light brown and rise to the surface.
Drain on kitchen paper and serve immediately.

Ratafia de cerises

—— CHERRIES BOTTLED IN *EAU-DE-VIE* ——

◇

The same method of preparation can be used for
other summer fruits – grapes, prunes or plums.
Morello cherries are best for this recipe. Remove
the stalks from 2 kg/4 lb cherries and leave the
cherries outside in the sun for 2 days. Wash them
well, and dry them. Half fill preserving jars with
the fruit. Add 10–12 cubes of sugar per jar. Cover
with *marc* (grape *eau-de-vie*). Seal the jars and
leave exposed to the sun for a fortnight. This way
the cherries will exude their natural juice into the
alcohol. The bottled fruit will then keep for ages in
a cellar or other dark cool place.

—— The Last Few Days: More Specialities ——

All too soon it was time to leave Corsica. By now I had toured the vineyards of the Cinarca region, the soft green meadows and orchards just south of Ajaccio, the cork fields of the Sartenais right down to the barren chalk of Bonifacio where only the hardy rosemary dares grow. I had sampled more regional specialities such as a succulent dish of red mullet and anchovies in Bonifacio, preceded by small aubergines flavoured with fresh basil and served with a highly spiced tomato sauce. With our coffee, some crisp dry biscuits, *fugazzi*, flavoured with white wine and *pastis*.

With a hamper full of chestnut flour delicacies and their respective recipes, provided by Ursule, I bade farewell to my friends in Vico to discover what must be the most breathtaking landscape of the island – from the bay of Sagone to the top of Cap Corse.

I followed the coastal road round the dramatic red granite landscape of Les Calanches, on to Porto and Galeria, a paradisical bay where young calves are left to romp on the beach. Then to the birthplace of Christopher Columbus, the imposing citadel of Calvi built by the Genovese, and just before the Cap, the charming port and market town of Ile Rousse. There, at the corner of the market square, I found a treasure trove of a food store. Every possible type of Corsican food was on display. Fresh, cured, dried, salted, cheese, meat or fish – it was all there. In the adjacent kitchen, three men were avidly eating some soup. 'Would you like to try some?' said the old lady, and this is how I discovered the Corsican *suppa di fasgioli rossi*, a soup of red beans served as a consommé with fresh pasta, to be followed by the beans eaten as a second course with bread and olive oil.

Above: Morning catch at Bonifacio.

Opposite: View of Cap Corse.

Rougets à la bonifacienne

—MULLET BONIFACIO STYLE—

1 kg/2 lb red mullet
6 anchovies in brine
3 tablespoons olive oil
1 tablespoon tomato purée
4 garlic cloves, crushed
2 large tomatoes
pepper
3 handfuls of fresh breadcrumbs
a handful of chopped fresh parsley

—— SERVES 4 ——

Preheat the oven to maximum.

Clean the red mullet and rinse the anchovies. Mash the anchovies to a paste with a little of the oil, the tomato purée and garlic. Spread in the base of an earthenware ovenproof dish. Cover with the tomatoes, thickly sliced. Lay the mullet on top and sprinkle with the remaining oil. Season generously with pepper. Mix the breadcrumbs with the parsley and scatter over the fish. Bake in the preheated oven for 30 minutes. Serve with a little rice and a side salad.

Suppa di fasgioli rossi

— RED BEAN SOUP —

750 g/1½ lb red kidney beans
2 tablespoons olive oil
1 onion, finely chopped
2 tablespoons tomato purée
3 garlic cloves
1 ham bone (optional)
salt and pepper
3 fresh basil leaves, chopped
100 g/4 oz tagliatelle

— SERVES 6–8 —

Soak the beans in water for about 3 hours.

Heat the oil in a large frying pan and soften the onion until transparent. Add the drained beans, the tomato purée and 1 garlic clove, together with the ham bone if used. Cover with 1.75 litres/3 pints water. Season with pepper and bring to the boil.

Reduce the heat and cook for 1 hour. Add salt to taste, the remaining garlic cloves, crushed, and the basil. Cook for a further 15 minutes. Spoon most of the beans out of the stock. Add the tagliatelle to the bean stock and cook for 6–8 minutes. Serve the soup, followed by the beans with a sprinkling of olive oil and plenty of black pepper.

Aubergines à la bonifacienne

— BAKED AUBERGINES —

10 fresh basil leaves
225 g/8 oz white bread
250 ml/8 fl oz milk
6 small aubergines
2 eggs, beaten
2 teaspoons clarified butter
100 g/4 oz grated cheese
(Parmesan and Gruyère or Emmenthal mixed)
salt and freshly ground white pepper
a little flour to coat
olive oil, for frying

SERVES 6 AS A MAIN COURSE
—— (HALVE QUANTITIES FOR A FIRST COURSE) ——

Tear the basil leaves into small pieces by hand, so as not to impair the flavour. Soak the bread in the milk, then squeeze out as much moisture as possible. Cut the aubergines in half lengthways and blanch in boiling water for 10 minutes. Drain well, scoop out the flesh and mix it with the bread, basil and all the remaining ingredients except the flour and oil. Sprinkle each stuffed aubergine with a little flour.

Heat some olive oil in a large frying pan. Place each aubergine upside down in the oil until golden-brown, then turn back on to the skin side, reduce the heat, simmer gently until tender.

Coulis

— SPICY TOMATO SAUCE —

◇

Simmer slowly the contents of a large can of peeled whole or crushed tomatoes with 1 tablespoon olive oil, 2 tablespoons tomato purée, ½ clove crushed garlic, a generous pinch of chilli pepper and plenty of freshly ground black pepper (for a variation of this *coulis* recipe see page 162).

Fugazzi

— DRY BISCUITS FLAVOURED WITH PASTIS —

These biscuits are traditionally eaten in Bonifacio on Good Friday. The quantity will vary according to the size of cutter used.

◇

500 g/1 lb plain flour
225 g/8 oz caster sugar
1 tablespoon vegetable oil
1 tablespoon dry white wine
additional caster sugar for sprinkling
a little pastis or Pernod for flavouring

— MAKES APPROX. 12 —

Sift the flour and sugar together. Rub in the oil, then add the wine to form a soft dough. Leave to rest for 1 hour.

Preheat the oven to 180°C/350°F/gas mark 4.

Lightly grease a baking sheet. Roll out the dough thinly and cut into round biscuits with a pastry cutter. Prick the surface of each one with a fork and sprinkle with a little caster sugar and a touch of *pastis*. Bake in the preheated oven for 10–15 minutes or until the biscuits are firm and golden. Cool on the baking sheet.

Right: Chestnuts: once the staple diet of Corsica, chestnut flour has almost become a luxury.

The Chestnut

◇

Although nowadays chestnut flour has almost become a luxury, chestnuts used to be part of the staple Corsican diet. Corn and wheat were hardly known and *la pulenda*, chestnut flour polenta, often replaced bread on the table. In certain villages it was the custom to serve 22 different dishes prepared with chestnut flour on wedding days, as well as other fresh chestnut dishes. The nuts were either cooked into a soup with the addition of wild fennel or roasted in a specially made vessel, *le testu*, a kind of flameproof basket with holes at the base.

La pulenda is still made from November onwards and eaten in thick slices either freshly boiled, grilled or fried. It is the ideal accompaniment to roast meat and game, as well as all pork products or even fried eggs. Over the years the Corsican housewife has also developed a good number of chestnut dessert recipes such as *a torta, e pisticcine* and *e nicci*, diverse tarts and cakes, and also a mealy fritter cooked in a shallow frying pan rather than deep-fried, *les fritelle castagnine*.

La pulenda

——— CHESTNUT-FLOUR POLENTA ———

Although the Corsicans use a special wooden fork for the making of their polenta, a whisk may be used. Just remember that the proof of the pudding is in the stirring.

◇

450 ml/¾ pint water per 225 g/8 oz chestnut flour
1 teaspoon salt

——— SERVES 6 ———

Bring the salted water to the boil in a non-stick saucepan. Stir in the chestnut flour. Stir for a further 15 minutes or so until the water is absorbed and the mixture is smooth.

Turn the *pulenda* on to a floured cloth. Fold the cloth around the mixture and shape into a ball. Remove the cloth and cut into thick slices.

To grill the *pulenda*, arrange the slices overlapping in a lightly oiled flameproof dish. Brush a little more oil on the top of each slice and grill until crisp and brown.

Le gâteau de Mina Colonna

——— CHESTNUT-FLOUR SPONGE CAKE ———

Use a 200 ml/7 fl oz cup to measure the ingredients for this recipe. Always make sure that the chestnut flour is double the volume of the milk and caster sugar.

◇

2 cups chestnut flour
1 teaspoon baking powder
4 eggs
1 cup caster sugar
4 teaspoons vegetable oil
1 cup milk

——— SERVES 6 ———

Preheat the oven to 180°C/350°F/gas mark 4.

Sift the flour and baking powder into a mixing bowl. Separate the eggs. Cream the yolks with the sugar. Add the sifted flour to the yolk mixture alternately with the oil and milk, beating thoroughly after each addition. Whisk the egg whites until stiff and fold them into the mixture.

Spoon into a greased medium loaf tin and bake in the preheated oven for 45 minutes or until the cake is well risen, spongy to the touch and the blade of a knife inserted into the centre comes out clean. Cool in the tin for a while, then turn on to a wire rack, and leave to cool completely.

—— The Last Port of Call: Centuri ——

The picturesque peninsula of Cap Corse is alive with fishing activities. On the Mediterranean side, each tiny cove deeply cut into the grey granite shelters a small fishing community. The translucent sea laps softly at the pebbly shore, the painted shutters of the old pantiled cottages match the colours of the fishing boats lined up on the strand, nets are strewn upon the rocks, a derelict fort or tower – a reminder of less peaceful times – stands erect at the harbour wall. In the midst of this arcadian setting, men and women spend their entire lives devoted to the sea. *'A chi dorme unpiglia pesci'* (who sleeps does not catch fish) goes the old Corsican proverb, The to-ing and fro-ing at the port of Centuri was ample proof.

I arrived in the early evening, and while what proved to be a magnificent *soupe du Cap* was being prepared by my host, I sat on the large balcony overlooking the port, drinking in the atmosphere. Nets were being dyed in a bath of rust and laid to dry on the rocks, boats were being painted or mended, unusually large lobster pots, *e nasse*, still handmade in Centuri with the supple wood of the myrtle, were piled on the small quay.

I heard the fleet leave in the middle of the night.

The next morning after a breakfast of bread, more fresh Brocciu and an unusual watermelon and pear jam, I explored the village. Predominant was that rich southern smell of tomatoes being cooked with so much garlic that it bites back. By a kitchen doorstep two women were talking. 'What is that delicious smell?' I ventured. *'Le coulis'*, they said, and explained that when the men return from fishing, whatever white fish had been caught that day would be quickly cleaned and simmered in the *coulis*, a fresh tomato sauce used for both fresh and salt fish in Corsica.

By the time the fishermen came back their wives as well as a good crowd of people, hoteliers and restaurateurs, were waiting. The wives helped unload the boats, and still using the old Roman scales, in no time at all sold the colourful assortment of fish and shellfish, including the prized *mustelle* fish, so fine in taste and texture that it is simply grilled or prepared *à la meunière* in a little butter. The *capone*, a brilliant red fish, would with the fine lobsters become a main ingredient of *u ziminu*, the Corsican *bouillabaisse*.

Above: Centuri, Corsica – lobster pots made with supple myrtle wood.

Opposite: Centuri – fishing nets laid to dry on the rocks.

Soupe de poisson du Cap

SPECIAL CORSICAN FISH SOUP

1 kg/2 lb mixed Mediterranean white fish,
such as John Dory, mullet, conger eel
3 tablespoons olive oil
5 onions, finely chopped
1 fennel leaf, finely chopped
4 large tomatoes, peeled and quartered
2 litres/3½ pints water
2 garlic cloves, crushed
1 large bouquet garni
½ teaspoon chilli pepper or ½ fresh chilli
2 teaspoons tomato purée
salt and pepper

TO SERVE
6 or more slices *pain de campagne*
olive oil
2 large garlic cloves, halved
75 g/3 oz freshly ground Parmesan

SERVES 4–6

Clean the fish under cold water, discarding the scales and fins. Pat dry with kitchen paper and cut into large chunks. Heat the olive oil in a large pan and soften the onions and fennel in it. Add the tomatoes and fish, sauté for a few minutes, then cover with the water. Now add the garlic, bouquet garni, chilli, tomato purée, salt and pepper.

Bring to the boil, then reduce the heat and cook for 45 minutes over medium heat, leaving the pan uncovered so that the stock reduces as it cooks. Spoon the fish and vegetables out of the stock. Discard the heads, bones, skins and the bouquet garni. Pound the fish and vegetables through a coarse strainer held over a soup tureen. This purée will thicken the soup.

Meanwhile, bring the stock back to boiling point and boil for a further 5 minutes. Pour the stock into the tureen, mixing well with the fish and vegetable purée. Check the seasoning.

Serve piping hot with slices of bread browned on both sides in olive oil, generously rubbed with fresh garlic and sprinkled with Parmesan.

Le coulis de tomate Corse

SPICY TOMATO AND ANCHOVY SAUCE

This is made with peeled ripe fresh tomatoes. Although the addition of a few anchovies makes it primarily the ideal accompaniment for fish, I have used this sauce successfully to cook veal. As in the Corsican meat sauce recipe it is essential to chop the shallots and garlic as finely as possible; they should melt in the sauce. The sauce is best prepared in a large heavy frying pan made of cast iron or copper; a good quality non-stick frying pan will do.

◇

2 anchovies in brine or ½ tin anchovy fillets
2 tablespoons virgin olive oil
2 purple shallots, very finely chopped
4 garlic cloves, very finely chopped
1 kg/2 lb tomatoes, peeled, seeded and chopped
1 large bouquet garni
pepper
a pinch of chilli or cayenne pepper
extra olive oil to finish

Mustelle fish – so delicate it is either grilled or fried and served with lemon juice.

Early evening in Centuri, Corsica.

If using anchovies in brine, soak them for 2 hours in cold water, changing the water once or twice, then pat dry. Heat the oil in a heavy frying pan, add the shallots and garlic and stir over medium heat until softened. Add the tomatoes, bouquet garni, pepper and chilli or cayenne pepper and stir well. Reduce the heat and leave to cook, uncovered, for 30 minutes, stirring from time to time.

Pound the anchovies to a paste with a little olive oil. Stir into the sauce and cook for a further 10 minutes. Check the seasoning.

Use the sauce over grilled white fish or add white fish fillets or pieces and a large glass of white wine to the sauce and simmer until the fish is flaky.

Confiture de pastèque aux poires

—— WATERMELON AND PEAR JAM ——

Pastèque, a colourful dark-skinned and red-fleshed watermelon is used for this recipe. The pears must be ripe but firm and flavoursome; Williams pears are a good choice.

◇

2 kg/4 lb watermelon
1 kg/2 lb pears
1 large lemon
2 kg/4 lb sugar

Peel and cube the watermelon. Peel and slice the pears. Finely grate the lemon. Remove the pith and cut the lemon into thin slices. Layer the three fruits in a large bowl, adding the sugar between each layer. Leave in a cool place, covered with a tea cloth, for 12 hours, in order to draw the juices out.

Transfer to a preserving pan. Bring to the boil quickly and boil for about 30 minutes or until the jam reaches setting point. Transfer to sterilized jam jars and seal well.

— CHAPTER 11 —

The South East

LYONNAIS · SAVOIE

From the bijou sophistication of a friend's apartment, I drank in the atmosphere of the second city of France: Lyons. Set between the Rhône and the Sâone rivers, once the exclusive domain of the silkworkers in a bygone era when Lyons was the silk capital of Europe, this vibrant city now lays claim to be the French capital of gastronomy.

Lyons' legendary passion for anything to do with the table was already praised by Rabelais when he sat Pantagruel in front of *godivaux* (meatballs in bouillon) and *cervelat* (brains) studded no doubt in true Lyonnais style with truffles and pistachio. Later, the great food revivalist Curnonsky spoke of the evidence of such gastronomic treasures in a city which is surround by the finest of France's raw produce such as Bresse poultry, fresh cream and wild mushrooms from the Bugey, cheese from the Dauphiné, game and freshwater fish from the Dombes.

Add to that the wines of the neighbouring *côte roannaise* and the great Beaujolais, the early fruit and vegetables grown in sunny orchards along the Rhône valley, and there is little choice but to bow to Lyon's epicurean splendours.

The Lyonnais can boast 30 or so of the greatest tables in France, where world-famous *chefs* contribute to the prime entertainment of the *gourmet* and the *gourmand*. For less exalted but no less authentic Lyonnais food, the visitor ought to explore the narrow streets of the old town and discover the cuisine of *les mères*, the formidable women cooks of Lyons. From the steamy depth of their matchbox-size kitchens they provide their customers with wholesome daily nourishment.

There, according to the time of the year or the freshest product gathered that morning, one will find intriguing specialities such as *tablier de sapeur*, a breaded tripe dish; *sabodet*, a coarse beef-and-pork sausage, also, a freshly cooked *saucisson* baked in a golden brioche.

Unabashed by such competition, the Lyonnais housewife seems totally knowledgeable and adventurous when it comes to good home-cooking. I followed my friend Simone to *Les Halles*, the covered market and large open-air food market along side the river Saône.

Loaded with smoked bacon, farm eggs, salad greens of all kinds, fish, cream and chocolate-coated petits-fours to have with coffee, we made it back to the black-and-white marble-floored kitchen with French windows opening into the *Vieux Lyon*. There, with great ease, Simone prepared a rich *saladier Lyonnais*, a large mixed salad served with tiny fried lardons and poached egg as a first course. It was to be followed by a delicate *escalope* of fresh salmon served with the creamiest of sorrel sauce. We then shared a Saint-Marcellin cheese *à point*, and to finish, a refreshing *compote des vignerons* made with preserved *pêches de vigne*, a small, bright purply-fleshed peach which is cultivated among the vine rows.

A courtyard in Lyons.

Saladier lyonnais

—— LYONS SALAD ——

To prepare this dish, be sure the eggs are absolutely fresh, for they need to be boiled for only 4 minutes before being left to cool and peeled.

◇

1 chicken liver,
poached in water and lemon juice and cooled
2 kipper fillets, marinated in oil and lemon juice
1 bunch spring onions, chopped
1 tarragon sprig, chopped
1 teaspoon chopped parsley
1 teaspoon chopped chervil
1 tablespoon red wine vinegar
3 tablespoons sunflower oil
pepper
100 g/4 oz dandelion greens
100 g/4 oz crisp lettuce leaves
100 g/4 oz lamb's lettuce
1 bunch watercress
100 g/4 oz cubed bacon *(lardons)*, sautéed and cooled
6 eggs, soft-boiled

—— SERVES 6 ——

Cut the cold chicken liver into thin slices and the kippers into 12 pieces. In a jug, make a vinaigrette with the spring onions, herbs, wine vinegar, oil and pepper.

Do not salt because of the addition of the kippers and bacon to the salad.

Layer the salad greens, liver, bacon and kippers in a large salad bowl. Add the vinaigrette. Check the seasoning. Garnish with the shelled eggs. Serve with crusty bread.

Escalope de saumon, crème d'oseille

—— THIN SLICES OF FRESH SALMON ——
IN A SORREL SAUCE

Ask the fishmonger to slice the fish diagonally and as thinly as possible, just as a butcher would prepare a veal escalope.

◇

200 g/7 oz sorrel leaves
150 ml/5 fl oz thick *crème fraîche*
100 g/4 oz unsalted butter
salt and pepper
6 salmon escalopes

—— SERVES 6 ——

First make the sauce. Blanch the sorrel for 2 minutes in boiling water. Rinse under the cold tap and drain well, making sure all the moisture has gone by the time you make the sauce. Pour the *crème fraîche* into a small saucepan, add half the butter, plenty of black pepper, salt and the sorrell, finely chopped or even better, puréed. Warm over low heat, stirring constantly until the sauce is thick enough to coat the back of a spoon.

Now cook the fish. Melt the remaining butter in a large frying pan. Sauté the salmon escalopes for no more than 2 minutes on each side. Season with salt and pepper. Spoon the sorrel sauce on to individual heated plates. Place the fish over the sauce and serve at once.

Compote des vignerons

—— PEACH AND GRAPE FRUIT SALAD ——

This dessert is best prepared 24 hours in advance and kept refrigerated.

◇

1 large bunch white Muscat grapes
300 ml/½ pint good red wine
300 ml/½ pint black grape juice
100 g/4 oz caster sugar
6 *pêches de vigne*, fresh or preserved
1 clove
1 cinnamon stick
pinch of freshly ground black pepper

—— SERVES 6 ——

Saucisson de Lyon.

Peel the grapes, using the point of a sharp knife. Discard the pips. Make a syrup by boiling the wine with the grape juice and sugar. When it starts to reduce, and becomes syrupy, add the grapes and peaches, peeled and halved if fresh. Poach the fruit in the syrup for 5 minutes with the clove, cinnamon stick and pepper. (If preserved peaches are used, drain them well and add them only at this stage.)

Carefully transfer to a bowl and keep refrigerated. To serve, discard the clove and cinnamon stick. Serve well chilled.

—— Les Dombes ——

I left the urban bustle of Lyons for the tranquillity of the lake region of the Dombes. There I was given an esoteric afternoon snack by a grandmother and invited to share a traditional meal and exquisite Grand Cru wines in the simple comfort of a farmhouse kitchen. I had encountered the relaxed hospitality of a Dombiste family.

The Dombistes do not regard themselves as Lyonnais or Burgundians. Their farming life is shared between the lakes and the fields. Culinary traditions are totally centred on the indigenous products: freshwater fish, frogs' legs, wildfowl of all kinds, as well as sweetcorn and farmyard poultry. The recipes used today are those of gifted farmers' wives, taught by their mothers and grandmothers. The dishes are simple, wholesome and unusual.

I certainly thought it was very unusual when my host asked if I would stay in one afternoon *parce que Grand-mère apporte le camion* – which literally translates 'because Granny is bringing the lorry'. The previous evening Grand-mère had been described to me as being nearly eighty years old, reserved, and jealously guarding a lifetime of family traditions. Somehow I was finding it difficult to reconcile this image with the now vivid picture I had in my mind of an eccentric French granny grinding to a halt in a huge lorry like some stuntman out of *The Wages of Fear*. I simply dared not ask any more questions and accepted the invitation.

By four o'clock Solange suddenly announced that she could see Granny making her way across the fields. I could not contain myself any longer and rushing to the window saw a plump little lady gently walking through the field, basket in hand. 'Where is the lorry?' I asked. '*Dans le panier*' answered Solange. She finally explained that *le camion* is the local name for the mid-afternoon snack of home-made garlic cheese.

We all sat down to this reviving speciality. With it, we drank *vin chaud*, warm red wine cut with a little water, lemon and sugar. Later on in the year, *le vin chaud* would be replaced by a refreshing dish of *socane*, strawberries or raspberries served in chilled young Beaujolais. Restored, the men went back to work. I stayed in with Solange and her mother-in-law, discussing Dombiste recipes and helping to prepare a traditional evening meal of *soupe à l'oignon gratinée*, followed by a *gâteau de foie de volaille aux quenelles*, an original combination of puréed chicken liver soufflé served at the same time as a dish of fluffy dumplings in a home-made tomato sauce. We finished the meal with a small helping of *roussettes*, small rum-flavoured fried pastries, and a lemony apple compote eaten lukewarm with a sprinkling of vanilla sugar. A 1987 Condrieu, followed by a 1979 Hermitage, were poured with panache by their *sommelier* son.

In the waterlands of the Dombes, culinary traditions are centred on freshwater products.

Le camion

HOME-MADE GARLIC CHEESE

500 g/1 lb *fromage blanc*
½ garlic clove, crushed
salt and pepper
a dash of red wine vinegar

SERVES 6

Mix all the ingredients together with a fork. Transfer to a deep earthenware dish. Keep refrigerated. Eat with crusty bread.

La soupe à l'oignon gratinée

ONION SOUP BAKED WITH CHEESE

To make a successful soup it is essential to prepare it in an ovenproof earthenware tureen which will then go straight from the oven to the table.

◇

50 g/2 oz lard or pork dripping
225 g/8 oz small strong-flavoured onions, sliced
2 litres/3½ pints veal or beef stock or salted water
6–8 slices of *pain de campagne*
100 g/4 oz butter
200 g/7 oz freshly grated Gruyère or Comté cheese

SERVES 6

Preheat the oven to 170°C/325°F/gas mark 3. Heat the lard or pork dripping in a deep pan. Sauté the onions until browned and almost caramelized. Add the stock or water and simmer for 15 minutes.

Meanwhile, toast the bread on both sides. Butter each slice and sprinkle with grated cheese.

Alternate the bread with the onion stock in an ovenproof earthenware tureen until it is three-quarters full. Reserve the remaining onion stock. Sprinkle the surface of the soup with more grated cheese. Place, uncovered, in the preheated oven for 1 hour, adding more stock if necessary. The soup should be bubbly and brown on the surface, leaving a smooth stock underneath. Serve piping hot.

Gâteau de foie de volaille

HOT CHICKEN LIVER MOUSSE

butter, for greasing the dish
2 chicken livers or 1 turkey liver
3 eggs
450 ml/¾ pint milk
60 ml/2 fl oz *crème fraîche* or double cream
¼ garlic clove, crushed
a handful of chives and parsley, finely chopped
salt and pepper
parsley sprigs, to garnish

SERVES 6

Preheat the oven to 170°C/325°F/gas mark 3.

Generously butter a 1.75 litre/3 pint soufflé dish. Using a blender or a food processor, purée the chicken or turkey livers, beat in the eggs, milk, *crème fraîche*, garlic and herbs as well as salt and pepper. Pour the mixture into the dish. Place in the preheated oven in a pan of warm water – the water should come three-quarters of the way up the sides of the soufflé dish. Bake for 30 minutes or until the blade of a knife inserted in the centre of the soufflé comes out clean.

Meanwhile, prepare the *quenelles* and the tomato sauce, as described in the following recipes.

To serve, spoon some tomato sauce all over heated individual plates. Carefully turn out a serving-spoonful of *gâteau de foie* on to the tomato sauce and lay a couple of *quenelles* beside it. Garnish with a little parsley.

Sauce tomate

TOMATO SAUCE

1 × 400 g/14 oz can peeled tomatoes, coarsely chopped
1 tablespoon tomato purée
a pinch each of chopped chives and parsley
salt and pepper
1 knob butter

Purée the chopped tomatoes in a blender with the tomato purée and herbs. Season to taste. Transfer to a saucepan and warm through gently, adding the butter towards the end.

Les quenelles de semoule dombistes

— LIGHT SEMOLINA DUMPLINGS —

2 eggs
16 tablespoons milk
100 g/4 oz fine semolina
6 g/2½ oz butter
40 g/1½ oz grated Gruyère or Emmenthal cheese

— SERVES 6 —

Separate the egg whites from the yolks. Warm the milk in a large saucepan. When just warm, throw in the semolina and stir constantly for 5 minutes. The mixture should thicken quite quickly – make sure the heat is not too high underneath the pan or the semolina will stick. Add the butter and mix well. Then add the cheese and mix well again. Leave to cool a little, then work the egg yolks in one by one. Whisk the egg whites until stiff and fold them in thoroughly. Keep the pan, uncovered, in the refrigerator for 1–2 hours.

To make the *quenelles*, boil a large amount of salted water. Using a dessertspoon, shape the mixture into ovals and lower carefully into the boiling water. The *quenelles* are cooked when they rise to the surface. Using a slotted spoon, transfer to a colander. Keep warm in the *Sauce tomate (see previous recipe)* until serving time.

Les roussettes

— RUM FRITTERS —

500 g/1 lb plain flour
3 large eggs
a pinch of salt
50 g/2 oz vanilla sugar
1 tablespoon dark rum
1 teaspoon grated tangerine or clementine rind
75 g/3 oz unsalted butter,
softened at room temperature
a bottle of sunflower oil for deep-frying
vanilla sugar for sprinkling

— SERVES 6 —

Sift the flour into a large mixing bowl and make a well in the centre. Break the eggs into the well.

Add the salt, sugar, rum, citrus rind and the butter in small pieces. Using the fingertips, mix the eggs and rum together first, then draw in the flour, working the butter in at the same time until a soft dough is obtained. Wrap the dough in a plastic bag and refrigerate for 3 hours.

Roll out the dough into an oblong. Divide into regular rectangular strips. Knot each strip in the middle with a single bow knot. Once all the roussettes are prepared, chill them on a floured baking sheet for 1 further hour.

Heat the oil in a deep-fryer. Place a small piece of bread in the oil; when it comes bubbling to the surface the oil is hot enough to deep-fry the *roussettes*. Fry them in batches until they are golden-brown on both sides. Drain on kitchen paper. Sprinkle with more vanilla sugar and serve with a fruit compote, a thick *crème anglaise (see page 43)* or a bowl of cold *crème fraîche*.

A farmhouse in the Dombes.

Opposite: Rustic kitchen furniture from the region.

—— From the Rhône Valley to the Savoie ——

Snow was melting on the rugged slopes, the *après-ski* haunts were closing their doors – the glamorous skiing season was over. I had left the wide Rhône valley in search of yet another aspect of French life – the life of the Savoyard mountain-dweller.

From Lake Geneva to the more southerly peaks, the clusters of small villages with their toy-town wooden chalets and churches, the numerous winding roads leading up to soft pastures and splendid views, the glittering icy ridge of the highest mountain in Europe, Mont Blanc, all seem utterly enchanting to the tourist. But just as the fisherman has learnt to respect the sea, the hardy *montagnard* has learnt to cope with this often treacherous landscape.

Today, even if they justifiably begrudge the appalling construction efforts of property developers, the Savoyards admit that the booming progress of tourism has helped ameliorate the harsh winter life – economically, of course, but also physically, as modern snow ploughs and wider roads have often put an end to a life of winter solitude under the silent clasp of the ice.

My hosts, just outside La Clusaz, were able to confirm this. Jean, now in his late fifties, was brought up on a cheese farm, and after precarious school days dictated by the rigours of winter months, became a shepherd. Today he is in charge of the local ski-lift. Yvonne, also in her late fifties, was brought up on a sawmill in a region bearing the evocative name of Les Terres Froides – the cold land. She now drives a small four-wheel drive car, but the lean, stooped figure, the rugged hands, the warm but sad eyes, are all proof of the strain of a harsh upbringing. They recalled the past when, during the winter months, people and cattle used to share the same roof for warmth. Their chalet, built entirely of wood, is a fine example of times past. It was built by Jean's grandfather and was once a cheese farm. The old dairy is still below the living quarters. The style of the chalet is particular to the region, with its wooden balcony running all round the first floor and the long pitched roof made of decorative wood tiles.

Inside, an ancient wood-burning stove glows in the main room, its two ovens always at the ready to gently bake or simmer a warming supper. The décor of the room is alpine: simple high-backed chairs, a calf's skin rug thrown on a wooden settle for warmth, and masses of artifacts hand-carved by the men during the long winters – cheese and butter moulds, pipes, ornate plates, pine cones, and a complete collection of mountaineers' walking sticks.

In this rustic décor an unassuming daily life is spent. Prime cuts of meat are seldom eaten, but the diet of the mountain folk needs to generate warmth. So huge gratins and bakes are often on the menu as well as thick soups made of salt pork and root vegetables. Cheese is probably the main source of protein. Local cheeses include Emmenthal, Chevrotin, Reblochon, Tommes, Beaufort and Vacherin. The list of savoyard dishes prepared with cheese is endless.

I was particularly intrigued by the recipes from Yvonne's native Terres Froides. Deliciously homely potato dishes such as *treuffes*, the *patois* name for potato truffles, or *grebons*, little fried potato croquettes prepared for Shrove Tuesday. One night for supper we ate a *gratin des Terres Froides aux saucisses*. With it, a salad made of shredded green cabbage and grated Emmenthal in a walnut oil dressing. We finished with *la Poutringue*, a kind of bread and butter pudding made with a rich compote of *quetsches*, the heavily perfumed local autumn plums. But before this I was made to try a local cheese concoction which would revive the dead: *le fromage fort*. This powerful delicacy – cheese matured in *eau-de-vie* – fully justifies its reputation!

Opposite: The rugged cliffs of Franche Comté.

Right: A hand-turned Reblochon cheese mould, still in use at the farm.

Le gratin des Terres Froides aux saucisses de kaion

SAUTÉED POTATO AND SAUSAGE SAVOY-STYLE

Kaion is the *patois* word for *cochon* (pig). This *gratin* made with herby pork sausages, potatoes and onions is easy to prepare and a welcome change from the usual *gratin dauphinois*.

◇

50 g/2 oz butter
6 meaty sausages flavoured with herbs
4 onions, sliced
150 ml/5 fl oz water
150 ml/5 fl oz white wine
1 kg/2 lb good waxy potatoes, peeled and diced
salt and pepper

—————— SERVES 6 ——————

Preheat the oven to 180°C/350°F/gas mark 4.

Melt the butter in a large flameproof *gratin* dish. As soon as it starts frothing, add the sausages and onions and sauté until golden brown. Add the water and wine, then the diced potatoes. Mix well. Season with a little salt and plenty of pepper.

Bake in the preheated oven until the potatoes are so tender they fall apart, adding more water if necessary during cooking. Serve with a green salad.

La poutringue

SAVOYARD BREAD-AND-BUTTER PUDDING WITH PLUMS

500 g/1 lb red plums, stoned
400 g/14 oz sugar
enough sliced stale bread, crusts removed,
to cover the base of an earthenware gratin dish
100 g/4 oz unsalted butter

—————— SERVES 6 ——————

Cook the plums with half the sugar and a little water for 50 minutes until a thick juicy compote is obtained.

Preheat the oven to 230°C/450°F/gas mark 8.

Butter each slice of bread and lay them at the base of a greased *gratin* dish. Cover with remaining sugar and bake until almost caramelized.

Spoon the plum compote over the bread. Place in the oven for a further 15 minutes. Eat warm with plenty of thick *crème fraîche*.

Les treuffes farcies des Terres Froides

— BAKED STUFFED POTATOES —

6 large potatoes
65 g/2½ oz butter
1 tablespoon oil
225 g/8 oz minced pork
1 onion, finely chopped
a touch of crushed garlic
1 teaspoon finely chopped parsley
salt and pepper
chopped parsley, to garnish

— SERVES 6 —

Preheat the oven to 230°C/450°F/gas mark 8.

Peel the potatoes and using a small sharp knife or vegetable corer, make round holes in them at regular intervals – they should almost resemble Gruyère cheese – but make sure to leave plenty of potato flesh in between. Place the potatoes without the stuffing in an earthenware roasting dish with the butter and oil. Cook in the preheated oven, basting well, until the potatoes start to take a good golden colour. Take out of the oven, leave to cool a little and reduce the oven heat to 180°C/350°F/gas mark 4.

Mix the pork with the onion, garlic and parsley as well as salt and pepper. Firmly pack this mixture inside the holes in the potatoes. Return to the dish and bake, covered with kitchen foil, for 40 minutes or until the potatoes are tender and the meat is cooked. Serve with a fresh sprinkling of parsley, and a crisp green salad mixed with 100 g/4 oz grated Emmenthal or Gruyère cheese.

Left: Spring in Savoie.

Right: A mountain dairy: Comté cheese.

Le fromage fort

— CHEESE MATURED IN EAU-DE-VIE —

A home-made cheese prepared with different cheeses and left to mature in alcohol. Each house has its recipe. Leave the *fromage fort* to mature in a cold place such as a cellar, for its pungency would impair the taste of other food if kept in the refrigerator.

◇

500 g/1 lb Reblochon cheese
6 spring onions with the green stalk, chopped
225 g/8 oz unsalted butter
salt and pepper
1 large dry goat's cheese
225 g/8 oz grated Gruyère cheese
150 ml/5 fl oz white *eau-de-vie*

— SERVES 6 OR MORE —

First slowly melt the Reblochon with the spring onions and half the butter. Make sure the mixture does not colour. Season with a little salt and plenty of black pepper. Transfer this mixture to a wide-top earthenware jar. Cover and leave in a cold place for 3 days.

Crumble the goat's cheese over the mixture and add the remaining butter and Gruyère cheese. Mash all the cheeses together to a paste. Add more pepper and finally work in the *eau-de-vie*. Replace the cover and leave to macerate for 3 weeks. Serve chilled.

— CHAPTER 12 —

Burgundy

'Burgundy – the art and pleasure of living' reads the traveller on all local guides, as he enters this favoured land. In a region where wine is king and where the products include prize-winning meat, the finest poultry in France, creamy cheeses and internationally renowned food specialities, the Burgundian is indisputably the *bon viveur*.

Once the most powerful state of West Europe, Burgundy today stretches from Champagne to the Lyonnais on one side and from the Nivernais to the foot of the Franche Comté mountains on the other, right down to the Bresse region and the Bugey hills.

Its map is riddled with inspirational names: villages such as Gevrey-Chambertin, Vougeot, Nuits St-Georges, Meursault, all bearing the name of their *grand cru*, and towns such as Dijon, famous not only for its *moutarde* and *crème de cassis*, but the seat of the International Food Fair for the last fifty years. There are many more evocative names: Mâcon, city of the national wine fair, Saulieu where every August the Charolais beef is prized at a renowned cattle fair, Marcigny, Louhans and Bourg-en-Bresse, centres of huge poultry fairs, and, of course, the ornate roofed town of Beaune where the Hospices de Beaune wine is still sold in the oldest of French style – by candle auction – each bottle reaching excruciating prices.

All this, linked with the names of celebrated gastronomes such as Brillat-Savarin and Pierre-François de La Varenne, could give the impression that Burgundy is the exclusive domain of French gastronomy. Although this is not the case, the region is dotted with unforgettable restaurants,

Early morning in Romanesque Burgundy.

and exquisite cuisine is to be found at the simplest of Burgundian tables.

Inspired by the abundance of food and wine, the Burgundian housewife masters rich sauces made to enhance the quality of each ingredient and match the subtlety of the wine. White wine is mainly used to simmer freshwater fish in *pochouse* or to prepare the fragrant *court-bouillon* into which the renowned *escargots de Bourgogne* will cook before being stuffed with delicately prepared garlic butter. Red wine enters the preparation of *sauce meurette*, a sauce made with tiny *lardons* and shallots. Eggs are poached in it and often served on their own as a first course or with light butterfly-shaped pasta as a main course. Another great favourite is *boeuf bourguignon*, generally made with a shin of beef and a wine of inferior quality to the one used for *coq au vin*, with which it is recommended to drink a wine at least as excellent as that used in the preparation. *Gougère* another Burgundian preparation. It is a cheese choux pastry which is either eaten on its own or filled with calf's kidney simmered in a red wine sauce. The gougère is then made in a large ring-shaped dish and the filling spooned at the centre.

To counteract such riches, other specialities are prepared in the plainest of fashions. There is *jambon persillé*, an aspic made of cured ham which has been cooked with fresh vegetables and wine vinegar and seasoned with shallots and parsley. It is then sliced thickly and served simply with crusty bread or a crisp salad. There is also *potée bour-guignonne*, the famous local pork and vegetable stew which, to be genuine, should be made without salt or spices. It was described as 'le génie dans un pot' by local author Gaston Roupnel . . . I found 'le génie' in the kitchen one early morning at Marcigny . . .

—— Breakfast at the Old Convent ——

Breakfast in France is usually a very simple affair – bread, jam and the occasional *croissant*. At her ancient converted convent in Marcigny, my doctor's wife's friend Josette Badin believes in a more sub-stantial start to the day. The *petit déjeuner rustique* she had prepared was very welcome as I was to spend the rest of the day roaming the ancient region of the Brionnais, discovering Romanesque Burgundy where the rolling green landscape is interrupted only by the handsome white figures of the Charolais oxen or the pale stone of some of the most beautiful churches in Christendom.

To cut the spring morning chill, a log fire had been lit in the vaulted whitewashed kitchen. On the imposing refectory table, locally handpainted gentian pottery, pewter coffee pots and sugar bowls awaited the breakfast guests. A single branch of apple blossom, still holding the morning dew, was laid simply against the waxed wood.

Freshly squeezed orange juice and steaming strong black coffee were poured as soon as we sat down, and the regal breakfast began. First was a cold *terrine de foie de dinde*, a smooth pâté. Purposely kept mild for this time of the day, with-out the addition of onion or garlic, it had been prepared with a hint of Marc de Bourgogne, the raw, grapey regional *eau-de-vie*. To follow, we were served individual delicate cheeses made with the freshest of goat's milk and dried in the cellar in a *chazère*, a small willow cage.

The last course was placed on the table straight from the oven. It was a golden crown-shaped brioche served with a sharp green tomato jam which had matured since the previous summer.

Above and opposite: Interior and exterior at the Old Convent.

Brioche de Josette Badin

— JOSETTE'S SPECIAL BRIOCHE —

20 g/¾ oz fresh yeast
2 tablespoons lukewarm water
350 g/12 oz plain flour
50 g/2 oz caster sugar
1 teaspoon salt
4 eggs, beaten
125 g/4½ oz unsalted butter, melted

— SERVES 6 —

In a small bowl mash the fresh yeast and lukewarm water to a paste. Add 75 g/3 oz of the flour and mix well to a soft, sticky dough. Leave to rise, covered with cling film, in a warm place for 15 minutes.

Sift the remaining flour, sugar and salt into a large mixing bowl. Make a well in the centre. Pour in the eggs and the melted butter. Mix the eggs and butter with a spoon and then draw in the flour. Just before it starts to form a dough, draw in the yeast mixture. Transfer to a floured board and knead well for 10 minutes. Transfer the ball of dough to an airtight vessel and leave overnight on the bottom shelf of the refrigerator.

The following day, place the dough on a floured board. Lightly flour a rolling pin and, starting in the centre, roll the dough into an oblong shape. Fold the rolled dough in 4 and roll out again into a large sausage shape. Cut into 8 regular pieces. Pat each piece into a round shape and place the 8 pieces side by side in a greased and lightly floured baba or savarin tin measuring 25–28 cm/10–11 inches in diameter tin with a hole at the centre. Leave the dough to rise in a warm room for 4 hours.

Preheat the oven to 220°C/425°C/gas mark 7. Bake the brioche for 45 minutes.

Confiture de tomates vertes

— GREEN TOMATO JAM —

Use large tomatoes picked just as they turn yellow.

◇

1 kg/2 lb tomatoes
1 lemon
1 kg/2 lb sugar

Chop the tomatoes coarsely. Slice the lemon and divide each slice into small sections. Layer the tomatoes and lemon with the sugar in a bowl. Leave overnight to draw out the juices.

Turn into a preserving pan, bring to the boil and cook until the jam is set, stirring constantly. Pot and seal. Keep in a dark cool place.

Terrine de foie de dinde

— SMOOTH TURKEY LIVER PÂTÉ —

If you can't find Marc de Bourgogne,
use any grape *eau-de-vie*

◇

600 g/1¼ lb turkey livers
2 tablespoons Marc de Bourgogne
pepper
500 g/1 lb pork belly
(reserve 5 thin slices to line the dish)
300 g/11 oz veal
2 eggs, beaten
15 g/½ oz salt
1 thyme sprig
1 large bayleaf

— SERVES 6 —

Leave the livers to marinate in the alcohol overnight with a pinch of freshly ground black pepper.

Preheat the oven to 180°C/350°F/gas mark 4.

Line the terrine dish with 4 thin slices of pork belly, rind removed. Reserve the 5th slice for the top of the *terrine*. Finely mince the veal and remaining pork, mince the livers (reserving the marinade), add the beaten eggs, salt and a generous amount of black pepper. Pour the liver marinade over the mixture, and work all the ingredients together with a fork. Spoon the mixture into the terrine dish and cover with the last slice of pork belly. Place the thyme and bayleaf in the centre. Cover the terrine.

Stand the terrine in a pan of hot water and cook in the preheated oven for 1½–2 hours. The terrine is done when it shrinks away from the sides of the dish, and the juices run clear. Leave to cool, with kitchen weights on top, and leave overnight. Keep refrigerated for 2 days before serving. To serve, either turn the terrine on to a serving platter or serve from the dish, cutting it into thick slices.

—— *La Potée Bourguignonne* and Other Family Recipes ——

En route to Mâcon, through medieval Burgundy, I stopped in St-Julien-de-Civry. The village was old and sleepy. In the square, a church, and a baker's shop which seemed to be the only centre of activity.

It was nearly lunchtime and, in true French style, children and husbands had been sent to fetch the bread while wives and mothers finished preparing the midday meal. Large round crusty loaves were pushed on to the back seat of old 2CVs, pressed against shiny blue overalls or strung on to bicycle saddles. A few more minutes and all one would hear through opened kitchen doors or windows would be the ritual sounds of *la France à table* – a pot being scraped, the clinking of knives and forks, and chairs noisily pushed back on stone floors.

As they left the bread shop, people were waving at the bright blue-eyed old lady who sat in the window of the shop next door. She was La Marthe, a young boy told me, the veteran of the village. Above the lace-curtained glass door faded gold letters read 'EPICERIE'. I pushed the door open and, to my surprise, stepped into a huge, totally empty grocer's shop. Only the fittings remained: two marble-topped mahogany counters, shelves, a large antique coffee grinder and a pair of brass scales as

polished and shiny as they would have been on opening day.

Marthe had retired many moons ago but obviously still cherished the surroundings which had been her *raison d'être*. She offered me a glass of home-brewed *cassis* and water and allowed me to flip through the yellowed pages of a well-used scrap-book. I learnt the plain truth about Burgundian cookery.

Above: The Epicerie.

Right: 'Lunch-time – husbands had been sent to fetch the bread.'

La potée bourguignonne

PORK AND EARLY VEGETABLE STEW

This dish should be prepared in the spring when all the new vegetables are available. It is best cooked for a large number of guests, for the more ingredients, the tastier the dish – remember, no herbs, no salt, no pepper.

◇

500 g/1 lb piece salt bacon
500 g/1 lb pork ribs, in one piece
1 pork hock
350 g/12 oz new carrots
225 g/8 oz leeks
225 g/8 oz small onions
225 g/8 oz small new purple turnips
1 small spring cabbage
500 g/1 lb small new potatoes, peeled
225 g/8 oz shelled petits pois

SERVES 8–10

Blanch the meats in boiling unsalted water for 10 minutes, then drain and rinse well. Place the meats in a large pot and cover with fresh water. Bring quickly to the boil, then reduce the heat and cook over low heat for 1 hour.

Wash and prepare all the vegetables, leaving the carrots whole and tying the leeks together in a bunch with some thread. Add all the vegetables to the pan except for the cabbage, potatoes and peas. Bring back to the boil, reduce the heat and cook gently for a further 45 minutes.

Divide the cabbage into chunks, add to the pan with the potatoes and cook for 20 minutes. Add the peas and cook for a further 10 minutes.

Serve the meat and vegetables together, pouring a few ladlefuls of stock over the dish. Eat with Moutarde de Dijon and large slices of *pain de campagne*.

Queue de boeuf Charolaise

BRAISED OXTAIL

100 g/4 oz unsalted butter
40 g/1½ oz lard
2 oxtails, divided into portions
3 large onions, coarsely chopped
2 carrots, cut into chunks
4 teaspoons plain flour

½ bottle dry white wine
1 small glass Marc de Bourgogne
6 ladles beef consommé
2 tablespoons tomato purée
salt and pepper
1 bayleaf
1 thyme sprig
500 g/1 lb small new potatoes, peeled

SERVES 6–8

Preheat the oven to 150°C/300°F/gas mark 2.

Melt the butter and lard in a large flameproof casserole and brown the oxtail thoroughly on all sides, together with the onions and the carrots. Sprinkle the flour over the oxtail, mix well and leave to colour slightly, then add the white wine, Marc de Bourgogne, consommé and tomato purée. Add salt, pepper and the bayleaf and thyme.

Cover and simmer in the preheated oven for 6 hours, or until the oxtail is thoroughly cooked and tender. Discard some of the surface fat.

Towards the end of cooking, steam the potatoes until tender. Transfer them to the casserole and leave to simmer for a further 10 minutes.

Meurette de pommes de terre

POTATOES SIMMERED IN RED WINE SAUCE

A simple, satisfying main course to be eaten with a sharp *frisée* salad tossed in a Dijon mustard vinaigrette.

◇

75 g/3 oz unsalted butter
12 pickling onions, peeled
1 new carrot, thinly sliced
225 g/8 oz salt bacon, cut into small *lardons*
½ bottle good red wine
1 bouquet garni
1 garlic clove
salt and pepper
12 medium waxy potatoes, peeled

BEURRE MANIÉ
1 teaspoon butter
½ teaspoon plain flour

SERVES 6

Heat the butter in a flameproof casserole or a deep sauté pan. When it starts to foam, sauté the onions, carrot and bacon until golden-brown. Add the wine, bring quickly to the boil and boil for 2–3 minutes. Add the bouquet garni, garlic, salt and pepper. Lower the heat and simmer, covered, for 20 minutes. Arrange the potatoes in a single layer in the casserole, cover again and simmer gently until the potatoes are tender.

Transfer the potatoes to a heated serving dish, and whisk the *beurre manié* (made by mixing the butter to a smooth paste with the flour) into the sauce. Spoon the *meurette* over the potatoes. Serve at once.

Haricots rouges à la bourguignonne

RED BEANS BURGUNDY-STYLE

500 g/1 lb dried red kidney beans
75 g/3 oz unsalted butter
2 onions, sliced
1 new carrot, thinly sliced
225 g/8 oz salt bacon, cut into small *lardons*
¼ bottle good red wine
3 ladles bean stock (*see below*)
1 bouquet garni
1 garlic clove

BEAN STOCK
1 onion, studded with a clove
1 garlic clove
1 bouquet garni

SERVES 6

Soak the beans in water for 2 hours. Discard the soaking liquid. Transfer the beans to a large pot and add the bean stock ingredients, with water to cover. Bring to the boil and boil steadily for 10 minutes. Reduce the heat and cook for 1½ hours. When cooked, drain the beans reserving some of the stock for the sauce.

Make the sauce following the instructions as in *Meurette de pommes de terre (see previous recipe)*. Add the bean stock at the same time as the wine. Add the drained beans to the sauce and simmer, uncovered, for 30 minutes. Check the seasoning and serve with plenty of crusty bread.

Le rigodon bourguignon

BURGUNDY BRIOCHE AND FRUIT PUDDING

A substantial country dessert served topped with a compote of stewed fruit in the autumn.

◇

600 ml/1 pt milk
100 g/4 oz caster sugar
1 teaspoon grated lemon rind
a pinch of cinnamon
100 g/4 oz leftover brioche (*see page 180*)
6 eggs, beaten
40 g/1½ oz plain flour
100 g/4 oz mixed walnuts and hazelnuts, chopped
25 g/1 oz butter

SERVES 4–6

Preheat the oven to 180°C/350°F/gas mark 4.

Bring the milk and sugar to boiling point, add the lemon rind and cinnamon. Leave to infuse for 5 minutes. Break the brioche into pieces in a bowl and pour a quarter of the flavoured milk over them. In a separate mixing bowl whisk the eggs and flour together. Add the flavoured milk gradually, whisking all the time. Add the softened brioche and the mixed nuts. Mix well.

Pour into an earthenware dish greased with the butter and bake in the preheated oven for 35–40 minutes. Serve lukewarm or cold with a compote of stewed fruit spread over the surface. I have tried it with stoned stewed plums, cherries and dried apricots. It is also eaten in the region with stewed apples flavoured with vanilla and a little lemon rind.

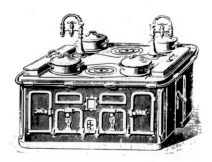

—— 'Le Weekend' in Burgundy ——

Just as I discovered that the new frontiers of Burgundy include the Bresse and the Bugey hills, it was not until I reached the weekend home of one of my relatives, near Bourg-en-Bresse, that I could truly appreciate the Burgundian art of good living.

My cousin inherited his vast Bressane house from an uncle who spent a meagre life in just one room. As if to make up for lost years, today the house is alive with family and friends of all ages.

Weekend open house in large French family homes is a great tradition. It is never a strain on the hosts as guests are expected to contribute. The weekend I spent there seemed a perfect rendezvous of gourmets and gourmands all eager to initiate me into the secrets of Burgundian cuisine. So, pen in hand, I followed this Epicurian whirlwind from cellar to kitchen, from store room to attic . . . from morning till night.

And as if that was not enough, my cousin insisted on driving me to Monet's *chocolaterie* in Bourg where tantalizing little nests of calories were purchased. Back in the kitchen, with many helping hands, family recipes were unveiled, revived and reproduced.

Above: A walnut oil press in Burgundy.

Cuisses de grenouilles à la bressane

— BURGUNDY FROGS' LEGS —

plain flour
36 frogs' legs
40 g/1½ oz butter
1 garlic clove
3 shallots, very finely chopped
salt and pepper
150 ml/5 fl oz dry white Burgundy wine
1 tarragon sprig
200 ml/7 fl oz *crème fraîche*

— SERVES 6 —

Flour the frogs' legs on all sides. Melt the butter in a deep sauté pan and sauté the frogs' legs with the whole garlic and the shallots until golden on all sides. Add salt, pepper and the wine. Add the tarragon.

Cook uncovered over medium heat until the wine has evaporated. Discard the garlic. Pour the *crème fraîche* into the pan and mix well with a spoon. Lower the heat and simmer until the sauce is smooth. Check the seasoning. Serve very hot with toasted slices of *pain de campagne*.

Escargots à la bressane

— SNAILS IN A CREAM SAUCE —

Escargots simmered in the same sauce as in the previous recipe. Serve them in individual earthenware ramekins with bite-sized pieces of toast spread with garlic butter.

◇

1 × 500 g/1 lb can escargots cooked in *court-bouillon*
40 g/1½ oz butter
3 shallots, very finely chopped
1 garlic clove
salt and pepper
1 glass dry white Burgundy wine
1 tarragon sprig
200 ml/7 fl oz *crème fraîche*

— SERVES 6 —

Heat the escargots in their *court-bouillon* in a saucepan while you prepare the sauce as described in the previous recipe.

Drain the *escargots*. Return them to the saucepan containing the sauce, pour the *crème fraîche* over them, mix well, check seasoning and leave to simmer until the sauce thickens. Serve with garlic toast.

Poulet de Bresse à la crème

— ROAST CHICKEN BASTED WITH CREAM —

Not the traditional chicken in cream, but roast fowl kept moist by constant basting with cream. The sauce is amazing. Try using an earthenware roasting pan; it will be even better.

◇

1 lemon
1 farm chicken with the liver
a handful of fresh parsley, finely chopped
175 g/6 oz unsalted butter
salt and pepper
250 ml/8 fl oz double cream
watercress, to garnish

— SERVES 6 —

Preheat the oven to 190°C/375°F/gas mark 5.

Halve the lemon and rub the chicken skin with it. Mince the liver and mix it with the parsley and half the butter, salt and plenty of ground black pepper. Spoon this mixture inside the chicken and secure the vent opening with a small skewer. Place the bird in a ovenproof earthenware dish and dot with the remaining butter.

Roast in the preheated oven, allowing 25 minutes per 500 g/1 lb. As soon as the chicken starts turning golden-brown, baste as often as possible with 2 teaspoons of the cream at a time.

To serve, carve the chicken and arrange the pieces on a heated serving dish. Scrape up all the pan juices, using a small hand whisk if necessary, check the seasoning and spoon the sauce over the chicken pieces. Garnish each piece with a small amount of stuffing and fresh watercress.

Lapin rôti à la moutarde

ROAST RABBIT IN A MUSTARD SAUCE

1 large rabbit, oven-ready
4 tablespoons Dijon mustard
1 bouquet garni
salt and pepper
4 rashers streaky bacon
2 onions
75 g/3 oz unsalted butter
150 ml/5 fl oz white Burgundy wine
200 ml/7 fl oz *crème fraîche*

SERVES 6

The day before, generously spread the rabbit inside as well as outside with two-thirds of the mustard. Push the bouquet garni inside the rib cavity. Season with pepper, wrap in foil and keep refrigerated.

Preheat the oven to 220°C/425°F/gas mark 7. Discard the foil and bouquet garni and wrap the rabbit with the bacon. Place in a flameproof earthenware dish, quarter the onions and place around the meat. Dot with the butter and roast in the hot oven for 40–45 minutes, basting regularly.

When the rabbit is cooked, carve it and transfer the pieces to a heated serving platter. Pour the white wine into the cooking dish, scrape up all the cooking juices with a spoon and add a little lukewarm water if the sauce is too short. Now add the *crème fraîche* and the remaining mustard. Over medium heat, bring just to boiling point, then spoon over the rabbit. Serve with a dish of small sautéed potatoes and a salad of *frisée* dressed in a shallot and wine vinegar vinaigrette.

A Burgundian kitchen.

Galette bressane

SPECIAL BRESSANE SWEET PASTRY

◇

Two *galettes* can be made with the following ingredients. The *galette à la crème* has thick *crème fraîche* and sugar spread on top. The other, made with the freshest of butter and sugar, is a *galette au sucre*. The Bressans eat it at any time of the day – for breakfast, mid-afternoon with tea or coffee or for dessert with a fresh fruit salad or a compote of stewed plums or cherries.

◇

15 g/½ oz fresh yeast
2 tablespoons lukewarm milk
500 g/1 lb plain flour
a pinch of salt
40 g/1½ oz sugar
100 g/4 oz unsalted butter
3 eggs

GALETTE À LA CRÈME FILLING
1 egg yolk mixed with a little water, to glaze
2–3 tablespoons thick *crème fraîche*
150 g/5 oz white or soft brown sugar

GALETTE AU SUCRE FILLING
1 egg yolk mixed with a little water, to glaze
50 g/2 oz butter
150 g/5 oz white or soft brown sugar

MAKES 2 GALETTES

Crumble the yeast into the milk in a small bowl. Mash with a fork and leave in a warm place for 15 minutes.

Sift the flour, salt and sugar on to a large wooden board. Add the butter cut into small cubes. Make a well in the centre. Break in the eggs and pour in the yeast mixture. Using the fingertips, work the central ingredients together first, then draw in the flour. Knead the dough for 10 minutes or until elastic. Leave to prove in a warm room for 2 hours.

Galette à la crème (Sweet pastry with cream)
Preheat the oven to 230°C/450°F/gas mark 8.

Return half the dough to a large floured board. Roll out the dough, starting from the centre, to a circle 5 mm/¼ inch thick. Transfer to a baking sheet. To avoid spillage of the filling, shape a small ridge all round the edge with the fingertips. Glaze the pastry all over with the egg and water mixture, then spoon on the *crème fraîche* and sprinkle the surface with the sugar. Cook in the hot oven for 15 minutes.

Galette au sucre (Sweet pastry with sugar)
Using the other half of the dough, proceed as above but replace the *crème fraîche* with the butter divided into 5 pieces and dotted over the pastry. Add a generous sprinkling of sugar. Cook in the preheated oven for 15 minutes.

Preparing the galette au sucre.

I visited a couple who press their own walnut oil – the wife gave me this delicious recipe.

Galette bressane aux noix

SWEET PASTRY WITH WALNUTS

◇

When the first walnut oil has just been pressed, the *galette* is garnished with cream, sugar, coarsely chopped walnuts and a sprinkling of walnut oil before being put in the oven. This *galette* is an excellent accompaniment to a fresh piece of Comté or Gruyère cheese.

— CHAPTER 13 —

The North-East

ARDENNES · CHAMPAGNE

Carved like a jigsaw piece at the centre of northern France, abutting the intricate frontier of Belgium, the Ardennes region is where the forest meets the industrial North. The region teems with game and an abundance of wild mushrooms in the autumn, when from mid-October it becomes a gastronomic paradise.

Around the feast day of St-Hubert, patron saint of hunters, it is impossible to find a spare table at any of the forestry *auberges*. Wild boar is a prime offering, together with venison. Game recipes abound, from roast saddles marinated in rich wines to tender *civets*. More specialized dishes include pigeon braised with peas, venison chops with wild mushrooms or fricassees with juniper berries. Cabbage is the vegetable of the region. It is either grated and served in a salad as a first course or more often braised with wine and small *lardons*. Red or white it makes an excellent accompaniment to the various game dishes. It is often stuffed with minced pork and served as a main course or boiled in a soup with a hock of country-cured ham.

For the region's ham is excellent. *Filet des Ardennes* is a delicacy to be found not only around the main city of Charleville-Mézières, but also in most respectable *charcuteries* throughout France. It is very mild, slightly sweet-cured, and is good on its own with bread and butter and a green salad. Used in cooking, it can be wrapped around a delicate crêpe, or used with a cheese sauce as a filling for a puff or choux-pastry.

It would be a pity to leave the region without trying the *tarte au sucre*, a delicate yeast pastry studded with sugar, served either for breakfast or in the afternoon with a strong cup of coffee.

South of the Ardennes lies Champagne. To appreciate the true magnificence of the *grand vignoble* it is best not to linger around the capital Reims, but to take the wine route to Epernay. There, as far as the eye can see, the autumn vine displays its richly coloured leaves. Each vineyard bears the name of a famous champagne house.

Although, as in any famous wine region of France, restaurants serve the finest of cuisine in the capital and the surrounding villages, the local cuisine is very *paysanne* and very simple: ham and pork products, *potées* and *matelotes* of river fish. For special occasions the Champenoise housewife will prepare the excellent and eye-catching dish of the region: *le coq en pâte*, a handsome cockerel stuffed with veal, pork and chicken liver cooked and wrapped in an elaborately carved puff pastry case. It will then be followed by a choice of the many cheese of Champagne. *Brie,* of course, mild, ripe and creamy all the way through but also the fine *Chaource*, or a *Cendré de Champagne*, a cheese of sharp flavour cured in wood ash.

I enjoyed two excellent meals in the region. The first was a small *repas de chasse* shared with friends in the Ardennes and the second, in Champagne, consisted of a good *salade au lard champenoise* with a glass of Bouzy, the red wine of the region.

The Ardennes – where the forest meets the industrial North.

—— *Le Repas de Chasse* ——

I visited a friend who married an Ardennais industrialist and lives in a solid white house, facing the river Meuse, outside Revin, in the north of the region. It was Michèle husband's shooting weekend and her turn to entertain the shooting party and their wives that evening.

We drank nothing but champagne and three regional dishes were served. First, a spicy *salade de chou rouge* made with dried fruit and nuts, already a taste of Eastern France. This was followed by *galettes à la viande* – individual meat and wild mushroom pasties. As a main course our hostess served pigeons braised in wine with tiny onions, peas and *lardons*. After a mustardy *frisée* salad and some cheese, we finished with pears poached in red wine, served chilled.

Salade de chou rouge

RED CABBAGE SALAD

1 large red cabbage
salt and pepper
wine vinegar
100 g/4 oz sultanas
10 dried apricots
10 prunes, stoned
15 walnuts
1 large cooking apple
sunflower oil
a pinch of ground cumin

SERVES 6

Twelve hours before serving the salad, wash the cabbage leaves, dry them and shred them finely. Place the shredded cabbage in a large bowl and sprinkle with a little salt and a dash of vinegar. Mix well and leave to marinate in a cool place or at the bottom of the refrigerator.

In 3 individual bowls, soak the sultanas, apricots and prunes in 2 teaspoon wine vinegar mixed with 3 tablespoons water. Shell the walnuts and peel and dice the apple. Drain the cabbage and dried fruit. Coarsely chop the apricots and prunes and mix with the nuts and apple in a large salad bowl. Make a dressing with 3 tablespoons sunflower oil, the cumin, salt and pepper. Pour over the salad. Toss and serve immediately.

Galettes à la viande

INDIVIDUAL MEAT AND
MUSHROOM PASTIES

500 g/1 lb puff pastry
milk, to glaze

FILLING
8 chanterelle mushrooms, coarsely chopped
25 g/1 oz butter
1 tablespoon port
100 g/4 oz cooked ham, coarsely minced
100 g/4 oz chicken breast, coarsely minced
100 g/4 oz raw Ardennes ham, coarsely minced
1 egg
1 tablespoon thick *crème fraîche*
a pinch of dried sage

a pinch of grated nutmeg
salt and pepper

SERVES 6

Sauté the chanterelles in the butter for a few minutes. Transfer to a large mixing bowl, add the port and leave to cool. Add all filling ingredients and work well together until the mixture adheres.

Roll out the pastry and divide it into 6 squares. Spoon some of the mixture into the centre of each square, piling it higher in the middle. Wrap up into small parcels. Damp the edges with a pastry brush and seal well. Place on a baking sheet, seam side down. Make a small hole at the centre of each pasty and insert a small 'chimney' made of rolled-up foil. Chill in the refrigerator for 30 minutes.

Preheat the oven to 200°C/400°F/gas mark 6. Bake the pasties for 15 minutes or until golden brown. Then lower the oven temperature to 180°C/350°F/gas mark 4. Cover the pasties loosely with foil to avoid burning and continue baking for a further 30 minutes or until a skewer inserted in the middle comes out very hot all the way. Serve at once.

Pigeons aux petits pois

PIGEONS BRAISED WITH PEAS

1 tablespoon oil
50 g/2 oz butter
225 g/8 oz bacon, cut into *lardons*
24 pickling onions, peeled
6 pigeons
150 ml/8 oz white wine
400 ml/14 fl oz chicken or veal stock
500 g/1 lb shelled peas
salt and pepper

SERVES 6

Heat the oil and butter in a large cast iron or flameproof casserole and sauté the bacon and onions until golden-brown. Remove from the pot. Brown the pigeons on all sides. Add the wine and stock. Return the onions and bacon to the casserole. Cover and simmer for 1 hour. Add the peas to the casserole and continue cooking for a further 45 minutes or until the pigeons are tender. Check the seasoning and serve straight from the dish with the cooking juices.

A Glass of Champagne and a Wholesome Salad

I was dying to try a *salade au lard champenoise*. In the Thiérache, my hosts had said, 'If you had stayed until tomorrow, we would have made you a real *salade au lard*.' Then I went to the Ardennes and heard the same story from my friend.

Happily, at the home of a cousin in the Champagne community of Mesnil-sur-Oger, near Epernay, I was told, 'You telephoned me at such short notice I had no time to prepare anything, so we'll have a *salade au lard*.'

We sat in the main room of her small *maison de vigneron,* drinking a bottle of the excellent champagne Blanc de Blancs Philippe Gonet, aged in the *caves* of the same village. In the fireplace, a log was burning slowly, and from the window all I could see was the landscape of autumn vines stretching into the distance.

Potatoes had been placed to boil on the stove, a *frisée* was washed and bacon cut into small *lardons*. The ceremony of the *salade au lard* commenced.

Simone warmed up a glazed earthenware saucepan on the embers inside the fireplace. She then peeled and sliced the potatoes into the warmed crock. The salad leaves were arranged over the potatoes and a lid put on the pan. She fried the bacon pieces for a short while and emptied the contents of the frying pan over the salad. Finally, vinegar and a tiny glass of Marc de Champagne were quickly added to the frying pan, with salt and pepper, and poured over the salad which was then tossed.

We ate it with crusty *pain de campagne* and a glass of red Bouzy. It was delicious and will certainly become one of my fireplace lunches.

Opposite: Inside the maison de vigneron in Champagne.

Below: Champagne countryside.

Salade au lard champenoise

— WARM POTATO AND —

FRISÉE SALAD WITH BACON

In the winter use *'frisée'*, in the spring freshly picked dandelions, and in the summer a firm Webb or escarole lettuce.

◇

500 g/1 lb medium new potatoes
salt and pepper
500 g/1 lb salad leaves
225 g/8 oz smoked bacon, cut into *lardons*
50 g/2 oz home-made lard
2 tablespoons wine vinegar
a teaspoon Marc

— SERVES 6 —

Boil the potatoes in salted water until tender but still slightly firm. Wash and dry the salad greens thoroughly. Fry the *lardons* in the lard. Then proceed according to Simone's method as described in the text above.

— CHAPTER 14 —

The East

ALSACE · LORRAINE

To voyage from Champagne through Lorraine into Alsace is to experience both bacchanalia and cornucopia. There is wine, beer and fragrant *eaux-de-vie*, and food so plentiful, so appetizing that even the most frugal would find it hard to ignore.

Major industries of the region are directly linked to the table – fine crystal at Baccarat, linen at Rambervillers and hand-decorated ceramics and stoneware at Longwy and Sarreguemines.

When I think of Strasbourg, the crossroads of Europe, I can see the magenta sunset over the cathedral, the reflection of the half-timbered houses in the Bain aux Plantes in the old quarter, and the bakeries displaying overwhelming quantities of breads, sweet and salted bretzels, almondy *petit fours*, huge kugelhopfs, cinnamon cakes, marzipan cakes, buns of all shapes and sizes, fruit and baked cheese tarts. And the *charcuteries* are filled to the brim with sausages and all kinds of pork and goose products, as well as mounds of pickled cabbage – *choucroute* – and lots of savoury pastries such as *kugelhopf* studded with smoked pork and walnuts, *flame-kueche* onion and cream tarts similar to the Burgundian *galette*, and large slices of *tourte de Munster*, fine pastry pies oozing with richly spiced meat.

In Nancy, the capital of Lorraine and a city of seventeenth-century splendour – especially around the Place Stanislas, a square designed by the last Duke of Lorraine, Stanislas Leczinski – I recall people queuing on a Saturday afternoon for freshly baked *madeleines*, macaroons and *baba au rhum*. At home these would be consumed only with home-made hot chocolate, another tantalizing speciality of Eastern France made by melting dark chocolate in milk.

And then, to cap it all, there is the traditional 100-kilometre trip along the wine route, through the picture-book villages and past the teutonic castles set among rust-coloured patchworks of vineyard. Once again the main attraction is the anticipation of chilled glasses of Riesling, the king of the Alsatian *terroir*, or Sylvaner, a lighter wine so easy to drink all through the day, or Pinot Noir, a fruity dry rosé. And then there is Muscat, the only dry French Muscat wine, excellent as an apéritif or with a slice of *kugelhopf*. Other famous wines of the region are the heady Tokay and potent white Gewurztraminer, which complements perfectly a slice of the strong local cheese, Munster.

Orchards set among farmhouses bring to mind the after-dinner crisp *eaux-de-vie* distilled from plums, mirabelles, pears, raspberries and wild berries, all very pure and dry, all very strong, all highly drinkable. I almost forgot to mention Marc de Gewurztraminer, a rival to the one of Champagne or Burgundy. It is all really too much to take, it seems to fit the way of life of the region so well. 'Cheerfulness comes from a well-fed stomach,' said Monsieur Rapp in Colmar, adding that in 1660 the people of Alsace were such big eaters that the police had to intervene and impose a penalty on excessive gluttony. 'We have had one

First winter snow on the Ballon d'Alsace.

thousand years of complex and troubled history; to compensate, we like to have fun and lots of celebrations.' They certainly do and the celebrations are all food-related. The calendar of festivals starts with St-Nicholas in December, then New Year's Day with the traditional brioche, the bakers' festival in February, and from spring to autumn homage to the cherry, fried carp, cottage cheese, the walnut, the turnip . . . to name only a few. People gather, eat and drink – the portions are large, appetites sharp.

Once again I was determined to discover, through local kitchens, recipes essential to the region but genuinely prepared for daily family needs rather than to satisfy tourists or to mark festivals. I wanted to get away from the banality of the *quiche* or *potée Lorraine*, the *choucroute garnie*, sauerkraut served with cuts of pork and various sausages found in every *brasserie* throughout France and in every *charcuterie*. I wished to avoid the *poulet au Riesling*, yet another dish of chicken cooked in a cream and white wine sauce. I was sure that other simmered meat dishes were prepared apart from the *baeckenoffe*, a substantial combination of meat and vegetables served in every *auberge* and *winstub*, the regional wine bar. I knew that the *kugelhopf* was king as far as cake is concerned, but I felt that others had to be discovered.

So, after a hearty breakfast in Lorraine of eggs baked with layers of smoked ham and cheese, I left my car one afternoon in the small village of Oberbruck and walked through forest and mountain paths until two hours later and 1,000 metres higher I found Ginette's farm tucked away at the foot of the Ballon d'Alsace mountain. As a mother of six, and conscious of preserving her family's culinary heritage, Ginette economizes by cooking according to the season, with products grown, reared and preserved on site. Within a few days I had been taught all the tricks of *la vieille Alsace à table*.

The Last Foray – a Farm Kitchen
—— in the Vosges Mountains ——

November 7. It snowed for the first time last night on the Ballon d'Alsace. For breakfast, Ginette has baked a fruity *kugelhopf*, the magnificent fluted yeast cake which is the pride of the region. It is standing at the centre of the kitchen table filling the room with an exquisite aroma of sweet spices. While my hostess prepares the accompanying hot chocolate I admire the simply laid table, the powdery landscape outside and, on the horizon, the crimson sunrise over the Swiss Alps. Suddenly it takes me back to the spring snow I had experienced in very similar surroundings in the Drôme in April – the same simplicity, the same warmth. The cake there was a local *pogne* which had been baked by Grand-mère. My culinary research was just starting then – and now, another few days and it will be over. It has taken the four seasons to rediscover my homeland; not only France but the French. People I hardly knew or did not know at all have opened their homes to me, let me share their daily fare, given away some guarded secrets. This morning, after twenty years away, I have the satisfying sense of still belonging.

A large bowl of hot chocolate has been placed in front of me and from now on gourmandizing will take over from contemplation. Only Minou, the house cat, has strategically curled himself by the stove and seems in full contemplation of whether

A few Alsace bread and cake specialities.

A working farm in Northern Alsace.

which is boiled with herbs and vegetables and served with a home-made horseradish sauce or used for the *suri ruewe* recipe, when it is simmered with pickled turnip, a preparation as popular as pickled cabbage. Ginette pointed to two enormous stoneware barrels where *choucroute* and pickled turnip were kept.

Fruit gathered in the family's orchard in the valley had already been dried and stored in linen bags for desserts of sharp *compotes* eaten with roast meat or game during the winter months. There were pears, apples, mirabelles and *quetsches*, large purple plums indigenous to the region. Haricot beans, onions and bunches of garlic were drying off beams, strings of small sweetcorn would provide animal feed. There was shelf after shelf of bottled fruit and home-made jams, as well as mounds of blueberries kept in the freezer. The slope facing the farm, which under the snow looked like pasture land bordering the forest, was in fact acres of blueberry bushes. Carp from the lake below is either baked whole with Riesling and a herb and mushroom stuffing, or filleted and deep-fried in a semolina batter.

Back in the kitchen we got out the pots and pans as well as numerous terrines and earthenware dishes. Rural cooking commenced – and lasted for three full days . . .

or not I will have the temerity to finish my breakfast. A lot of food preparation is on the agenda, for Ginette, whose children have now grown up and left home, opens her house to ramblers exploring the Ballon d'Alsace and its surrounding lakes and valleys. She is never too sure how many people she will have to feed but she always copes.

It was wonderful to visit the farm and share the realities of self-sufficient mountain life. A trip to the village is quite an expedition, especially during the winter months. When the snow is at its deepest the family is totally cut off, and so from spring onwards each task counts towards winter comfort later on. Logging and looking after the animals seems to be Paul's task while Ginette assiduously stocks the food store-room, as well as baking the bread weekly and making cream and butter.

I was bewildered by the sight of the store-room. Giant smoked and cured hams were hanging from the beams together with *schwinawischt*, a solid sausage which is boiled and served in chunks in a thick vegetable soup. There was *kassler*, a delicate smoked pork fillet – once dried it is thinly sliced and eaten cold with various salads, or quickly fried in butter and served with vegetables or *choucroute*. There was *schifala*, a smoked shoulder of pork

Right: Sweetcorn – the winter food for free-range poultry at Le Gresson farm in Alsace.

First, a few main dishes and their accompaniment.

Surlewerla mit knœpfle

— LIVER WITH NOODLES —

Cubes of pig's liver cooked in a wine sauce and served with home-made fresh noodles – *knoepfle*.

◇

KNOEPFLE

275 g/10 oz plain flour
½ teaspoon salt
3 eggs
1 tablespoon milk, more if necessary
1 knob butter

SURLEWERLA

½ teaspoon sunflower oil
75 g/3 oz butter
4 shallots, finely chopped
40g /1½ oz plain flour
200 ml/7 fl oz Alsace white wine
200 ml/7 fl oz red wine
2 teaspoons wine vinegar
1 whole garlic clove
1 fresh bouquet garni
2 juniper berries, crushed
a touch of grated nutmeg
1 clove
salt and pepper
500 g/1 lb pig's liver
1 tablespoon lard

— SERVES 4–6 —

Prepare the noodles by sifting the flour and salt on to a large wooden board. Make a well in the centre. Break the eggs into the well and using the fingertips, slowly work the flour with the eggs adding a little milk at a time until the dough is soft. Knead it with the palms of the hands until very smooth and leave to rest for at least 1 hour.

To cook the noodles, bring a large pan of salted water to the boil. Meanwhile, using a very small teaspoon dipped each time in boiling water, spoon up equal amounts of dough and roll into small oblong sticks with the fingertips. Cook in boiling water for 8 minutes. Drain well. Place the butter in a heated serving dish, transfer the noodles to it, toss well and serve as an accompaniment to the Surlewerla which is prepared as follows.

Heat the oil and butter in a sauté pan and sauté the shallots until golden but not brown. Sprinkle the flour over the shallots and mix well with a wooden spatula. Let the flour take colour, then pour in the two wines and the vinegar, mixing well. Reduce the heat to a minimum, then add the garlic, bouquet garni and spices. Cover and simmer the sauce gently for 20 minutes. If it reduces too much add a little lukewarm water.

Meanwhile, cut the liver into small regular cubes. Heat the lard in a frying pan and sauté the liver for about 8 minutes until brown on all sides: it should be slightly pink in the middle although cooked all the way through. Transfer the liver to the sauce and check the seasoning. To serve, discard the garlic, bouquet garni, clove and juniper berries from the sauce. Spoon the sauce into a serving dish and serve with the noodles.

The faïence and copper of Alsace – most cakes are baked in earthenware.

Fleischschnacka

MINCED MEAT PARCELS
IN A PASTA CASING

The traditional Monday meal of boiled beef and chicken. It can be prepared with leftover *pot au feu*, i.e. beef only. Just make sure you keep some meat stock for the sauce.

◇

NOODLE DOUGH
275 g/10 oz plain flour
200 g/7 oz fine semolina
6 eggs
1 tablespoon water, if necessary

FILLING
1 kg/2 lb leftover mixed boiled beef and chicken, finely minced
1 onion, finely chopped
1 shallot, finely chopped
1 garlic clove, crushed
1 tablespoon finely chopped parsley
a little thyme
1 egg
salt and pepper
a little plain flour, to coat
1 tablespoon sunflower oil and 40 g/1½ oz butter, for frying

SAUCE
1 glass Alsace white wine
½ glass red wine
500 ml/18 fl oz meat stock

SERVES 6

To make the noodles, sift the flour and semolina on to a large wooden board. Make a well in the centre. Beat the eggs gently and pour into the well. Using the fingertips, draw the flour mixture into the eggs until a dough is formed, adding water if necessary.

Lightly flour the board and using the palms of your hands knead the dough for 10 – 15 minutes until smooth and elastic. Shape the dough into a ball. Cover with a cloth and leave to rest for 2 hours. Now roll out the dough thinly (2–3 mm/ 1⅛ inch) into a rectangle. Attach a long piece of string between two chairs, hang the dough carefully over it and leave to dry for 2 hours.

To make the filling, mix all the ingredients together and check the seasoning. Spread the mixture all over the noodle dough and roll up like a Swiss roll. Moisture the edges and press with the fingers to seal well. Cut the roll into even slices. Lightly flour each slice.

Heat the oil and butter in a deep sauté pan and sauté the slices until golden but not brown. Add the two wines and the stock. Cover and simmer very gently for 1 hour.

A few mushrooms may be added 15 minutes before serving. Serve with a dish of *Pommes de terre des montagnes (recipe follows)* and a green salad.

Pommes de terre des montagnes

POTATOES PURÉED WITH
FENNEL LEAVES AND GARLIC

1 kg/2 lb large floury potatoes
2 tablespoons *crème fraîche*
50 g/2 oz butter
a touch of crushed garlic
1 teaspoon finely chopped fennel leaves or, even better, wild fennel
salt and pepper

SERVES 6

Boil the potatoes, drain well and mash with the other ingredients. Check the seasoning and serve at once.

A corner of the store-room in Ginette's farm.

The woodcutter's luncheon

— POTATOES AND SWEDES —
SAUTÉED WITH SMOKED BACON

A simple meal served on the farms
during the cold months.

◇

500 g/1 lb waxy potatoes
500 g/1 lb swedes
100 g/4 oz butter
100 g/4 oz home-made lard
or 1–2 tablespoons sunflower oil
175 g/6 oz smoked streaky bacon, diced
3 onions, finely chopped
pepper
a little grated nutmeg
salt (optional)

— SERVES 6 —

Cut the peeled potatoes and swedes into even
cubes and parboil them. Drain well. Heat the
butter and lard or oil in a cast iron frying pan.
Sauté the bacon with the onions until they start to
colour. Add the well-drained vegetables, pepper
and nutmeg. Sauté until everything is golden-
brown, reduce the heat and simmer, covered, until
the vegetables are tender. Shake the pan from time
to time so that the mixture does not stick to the
pan. Check the seasoning and serve at once with
thick slices of *pain de campagne*, accompanied by a
chilled Riesling.

Boeuf Gresson

— WINTER BEEF STEW —

Marinated cubes of beef cooked
in an earthenware terrine

◇

1 kg/2 lb chuck steak, diced
½ bottle Riesling or Sylvaner
2 carrots, sliced
2 leeks, sliced
2 onions, sliced
2 garlic cloves

¼ teaspoon ground cloves
1 bouquet garni
2 tablespoons oil
25 g/1 oz butter
4 large tomatoes, peeled but left whole
100 g/4 oz mushrooms, sliced

— SERVES 6–8 —

Marinate the meat for 24 hours with the wine,
carrots, leeks, onions, garlic, spice and bouquet
garni.

The following day, lift the meat cubes out of the
marinade and dry with kitchen paper. Reserve the
entire marinade. Sauté the meat cubes in a mixture
of the oil and butter until brown on all sides.

Preheat the oven to 170 °C/325 °F/gas mark 3.
Layer the meat and vegetables from the marinade
inside a glazed earthenware terrine. Pour in the
marinade and a little water so that the ingredients
are completely covered. Place the lid over the
terrine and cook gently in the preheated oven for
2¾ hours.

Add the tomatoes and mushrooms and cook for
a further 45 minutes or until the tomatoes seem
well cooked and have gone mushy. Serve straight
from the terrine with boiled potatoes and a winter
salad.

Salade d'hiver

— WINTER SALAD —

1 small white cabbage
1 small red cabbage
2 turnips
3 carrots
salt
wine vinegar

DRESSING
2 tablespoons sunflower or walnut oil
2 teaspoons *crème fraîche*
1 teaspoon mustard
a pinch of cumin
white pepper

— SERVES 6–8 —

Two hours before serving the salad, shred the
white and red cabbage finely and grate the turnips
and carrots coarsely. Using 4 individual bowls,

leave the vegetables to marinate separately in salt and a little vinegar.

When ready to serve drain off any liquid from the vegetables. Place them all in a salad bowl. Whisk together the dressing ingredients, add to the vegetables and toss well. Check the seasoning and add a little more vinegar if necessary, as well as a touch of ground white pepper. Serve at once.

Galriawler met spack

— PORK STEW WITH CARROTS AND TURNIPS —

Another country winter dish which once again benefits from simmering slowly in an earthenware terrine or oblong earthenware casserole dish. Ginette served it with mashed potatoes.

2 tablespoons sunflower oil
2 garlic cloves, chopped
4 shallots, sliced
1 teaspoon ground bayleaf
a pinch of ground cloves
2 teaspoons ground coriander
salt and pepper
1 kg/2 lb lean pork, cubed
275 g/10 oz carrots
275 g/10 oz turnips
freshly chopped parsley

— SERVES 6–8 —

The previous day, combine 1 tablespoon of the oil with the garlic, shallots, bayleaf, cloves, coriander and pepper. Place the pork in a bowl and mix with the spice mixture until thoroughly coated. Cover and leave in a cold place or in the refrigerator.

The following day, preheat the oven to 180 °C/ 350 °F. gas mark 4. Heat the remaining oil in a cast iron pan and sauté the spiced meat until golden brown on all sides. Transfer to an earthenware terrine and cover with warm water. Place the lid on the terrine and cook in the preheated oven for 2 hours until the meat is tender.

Meanwhile dice the carrots and turnips and cook them in boiling salted water until tender. Drain well. Fifteen minutes before serving, add them to the terrine and return to the oven. Serve straight from the terrine with a sprinkling of chopped parsley.

Les tartes alsaciennes

— SAVOURY AND FRUIT TARTS —

◇

All through the Eastern region, starting with the 'quiche' in Lorraine, tarts are a great speciality. We begin with a classic savoury tart recipe, followed by three dessert recipes. The fruit *tarte alsacienne*, which is an almost daily dessert in Alsace, is a pastry-based open tart, topped with apples, plums, cherries, blueberries, mirabelles or pears, over which is poured a sweet custardy mixture. Sometimes ground almonds or spices are added but it is generally always the same formula. Such tarts are at their best eaten lukewarm when the fruit flavour has had time to ooze through the baked custard.

Tarte aux poireaux

— LEEK TART —

At 'Le ferme des Gressons' my cordon bleu friend baked an exceptional leek tart for lunch one day. I found it far superior to onion tart, which always tends to be rather sweetish, whichever onions are used. This was light and very vegetably and will figure frequently on my menus.

PASTRY
225 g/8 oz plain flour
100 g/4 oz salted butter
1 small glass iced water

FILLING
600 g/1¼ lb leeks
1 onion
40 g/1½ oz butter
100 g/4 oz smoked streaky bacon, cut very thinly
2 egg yolks
1 teaspoon cornflour
300 ml/½ pint *crème fraîche*
150 g/5 oz grated Gruyère cheese
salt and pepper
a touch of grated nutmeg

— SERVES 6 —

To make the pastry, sift the flour on to a large wooden board. Cut the butter into small pieces and dot them all over the flour. Make a well in the centre and pour in the iced water. Working quickly with cool floured fingertips, work the butter into the flour, then draw the butter and flour into the water until a smooth dough is formed. Knead 2–3 times with the palms of your hands, and shape into a ball and leave for at least 1 hour. If small pieces of butter are dotted in the pastry it does not matter.

Preheat the oven to 190 °C/375 °F, gas mark 5.

Roll out the pastry and use to line a 30 cm/12 inch tart dish.

Trim the leek and discard the toughest green leaves, leaving as much green as possible. Wash the leeks carefully under cold running water and slice them downwards and across into oblong pieces. Peel and thinly slice the onion.

Place the butter in a large saucepan, cover with the leeks and onions and leave the vegetables to sweat over a low heat, stirring from time to time, until they are almost tender and the liquid has evaporated. Now add the bacon, cut into small pieces and cook for a further 5–6 minutes until the bacon is transparent.

Meanwhile, beat the egg yolks with the cornflour and *crème fraîche*. Add the grated cheese, salt, pepper and nutmeg. Make sure that there is no liquid left in the leek and bacon pan, then add the *crème fraîche* and egg mixture away from the heat. Mix well and check the seasoning. Pour the mixture into the pastry case and bake in the preheated oven for 30 minutes. Serve immediately, on its own, as a first course. This tart does not benefit from being made in advance then reheated.

Tarte aux pommes alsacienne

———————— ALSACE-STYLE APPLE TART ————————

Being used to my Normandy *tarte aux pommes* made with thinly sliced apples I was fascinated by the way Ginette dealt with hers, and found the result equally delicious.

◇

PÂTE BRISÉE SUCRÉE (SWEET SHORTCRUST PASTRY)
225 g/8 oz plain flour
a pinch of salt
25 g/1 oz caster sugar

100 g/4 oz unsalted butter
1 egg
a little iced water

FILLING
1 kg/2 lb large dessert apples
a little ground cinnamon
100 g/4 oz caster sugar
100 ml/4 fl oz *crème fraîche*
1 tablespoon milk
2 eggs
icing sugar for sprinkling

———————— SERVES 6 ————————

To make the pastry, sift the flour salt and sugar onto a large wooden board. Dot small pieces of butter over the flour. Make a well in the centre and add the egg. With cool floured fingertips, working quickly, rub the butter into the flour and then draw into the egg, adding a little iced water if necessary until a smooth dough has been obtained. Knead 2–3 times with the palms of the hand. Shape into a ball and leave to rest for at least 30 minutes before rolling out.

Preheat the oven to 190 °C/375 °F, gas mark 5.

Roll out the pastry and use to line a 30 cm/12 inch tart dish.

Peel the apples and divide them in quarters. Make criss-cross incisions on each quarter to facilitate cooking and arrange the fruit on the dough, rounded side up. Sift the cinnamon with half the caster sugar and sprinkle over the fruit. Bake in the preheated oven for 20 minutes.

Meanwhile, beat together the *crème fraîche*, milk and eggs with the remaining caster sugar. Pour over the tart and bake for a further 20–25 minutes, or until the mixture is set and golden-brown. Allow to cool, then sprinkle with icing sugar.

Tarte aux poires

———————— PEAR TART ————————

◇

Proceed exactly as above but it is excellent to add 1 teaspoon *Poire eau-de-vie* to the custard as well as 1 heaped tablespoon ground almonds. It is also recommended to sprinkle a few fine breadcrumbs over the dough so that any juice from the pears is absorbed and the pastry is kept dry.

Preparing the tarte alsacienne.

Finally one afternoon, at my request, we made a batch of *schenkele*. I was a child the last time I ate these little almondy fingers, perfumed with Kirsch and finely grated lemon rind. A friend of my mother used to serve them with the finest of china tea. She was very *vieille France* and to this day, I remember the Louis XV salon, the fine teacups, the hand-laced serviettes, the portrait of a lady who looked like Marie-Antoinette above the fireplace and the exquisite pleasure of biting into the spicy little sticks. The revived taste was no disappointment and I am so happy to have the recipe now.

Schenkele

ALMOND BISCUITS

These keep for a few days in an airtight tin and are good cold.

◇

225 g/8 oz caster sugar
4 eggs
500 g/1 lb plain flour
100 g/4 oz unsalted butter
100 g/4 oz ground almonds
finely grated rind of ½ a lemon
a small pinch of salt
1 tablespoon Kirsch
sunflower oil for deep-frying
extra caster sugar, for coating

MAKES 20–24

Cream the sugar and eggs in a mixing bowl until light and frothy. Whisk in the flour, melted butter, ground almonds, lemon rind, salt and Kirsch, until a smooth dough is obtained. Shape the dough into a large ball and leave to rest for 2 hours.

Transfer the dough to a floured wooden board, cut it into large chunks and using floured fingertips, take small pieces from each section and roll into individual sticks the shape and size of a small sausage. Heat fresh oil in a deep-fryer. Place a small cube of bread in the oil – as soon as it rises to the surface, the oil is hot enough.

Deep-fry the *Schenkele* for 4 minutes or until golden but not brown. Drain well and pat dry on kitchen paper. While still warm, roll each *Schenkele* in some caster sugar which can be mixed with a little cinnamon if liked. Eat lukewarm or cold.

Tarte aux myrtilles

BLUEBERRY TART

I have sampled two versions of this tart and personally am not very keen on cooking the blueberries with the custard mixture – partly because it impairs the sharp juiciness of the fruit, but mainly because the custard takes on the dark colour of the fruit and the visual result is not particularly appetizing.

◇

225 g/8 oz *Pâte brisée sucrée*
(see *Apple tart recipe, page 202*)
1 kg/2 lb blueberries
2 tablespoons caster sugar

SERVES 6

Line the dish with pastry, spoon the fruit over it, sprinkle with half the sugar and bake at 190°C/375°F, gas mark 5.

Sprinkle with the remaining sugar once the tart is cooked. Eat lukewarm or cold.

List of Recipes